W9-ATN-104

EDWARD KOIKI MABO

Professor Noel Loos teaches the history of black–white relations in Australia at James Cook University in Townsville. Currently completing a study of Aboriginal mission history, he has conducted research into frontier conflict, the place of Aborigines in colonial society, and the evolution of government policies for Aboriginal and Torres Strait Islander people. In the 1970s he pioneered the development of teacher education programs in Queensland for Aboriginal and Islander people.

A friend of Koiki Mabo for 25 years, Professor Loos has published widely on indigenous history and politics, including: *Invasion and Resistance: Aboriginal–European Relations on the North Queensland Frontier 1861–1897* (ANU Press, 1982), *Succeeding Against the Odds: Townsville's Aboriginal and Islander Teacher Education Program* (edited with Greg Miller) (Allen & Unwin, 1989) and *Indigenous Minorities and Education: Australian and Japanese Perspectives of their Indigenous Peoples, the Ainu, Aborigines and Torres Strait Islanders* (edited with Takeshi Osanai) (Sanyusha Publishing Co., Tokyo, 1993).

EDWARD KOIKI MABO

His life and struggle for land rights

Noel Loos and Koiki Mabo

University of Queensland Press

First published 1996 by University of Queensland Press
Box 42, St Lucia, Queensland 4067 Australia

Typeset by University of Queensland Press
Printed in Australia by McPherson's Printing Group

Distributed in the USA and Canada by
International Specialized Book Services, Inc.,
5804 N.E. Hassalo Street, Portland, Oregon 97213-3640

Cataloguing in Publication Data
National Library of Australia

Loos, Noel.
  Koiki Mabo.

    1. Mabo, Eddie, 1936–1992. 2. Aborigines, Australian —
  Biography. I. Title.

305.89915092

ISBN 0 7022 2905 9

To my daughter Anne Loos
and to Netta Mabo,
two strong women

Dad obviously thinks
all my working out
has paid off.
Happy Reading.
Love
Anne Loos.

Glossary to 'Who Was That Boy'

The poem opposite was delivered by Commissioner George Mye MBE at a United Nations Working Group on Indigenous Populations in Geneva, Switzerland in July 1995

op magerr: area of garden land above the beaches leading up to the hills.
sisi: walking up a coconut tree with hands and legs goanna-style not frog-style.
apek kebile: the little boy from the far side of the island (*apek:* the other side; *kebile:* a small boy).
lamar: ghost, spirit. It could also refer to Europeans because of their pale skins.
lug-le: sorceror (the greatest fear of Islanders even today).
zogo: sacred power.
arerr: ancestors.
waitai: the music created by the wind on bamboo fences erected as windbreaks.
maiso: the constant roar or rumbling of the waves on the nearby Great Barrier Reef; sound of the surf.
toli: small brown birds, 'sandpipers'.
em-oot (more usually *oot-em*): for sleep; while you sleep.
puar: vine.
puar amissir-amissir: a vine climbing round and round up a coconut tree. It is totemically significant, especially to Koiki Mabo's Piadram clan at Las.

WHO WAS THAT BOY

I knew him as a child of Islander birth, at home
on a beautiful island, the jewel of the Coral Sea
Frolicking on beaches and *op magerr* he loved to roam
or mastering — the art of *sisi* on the tallest coconut tree

Who was that boy

Apek kebile for all his tender years
Trekking the miles to school was always a familiar sight
Of *lamar* and *lug-le* he boasted no fears
The *zogo* of his *arerr* he trusted and clinged to with might

Who was that boy

Some ventured that David was his name
Others were in doubt as it was spelt with "K"
Pebble however small has traded them both to fame
Dearly though the price that he had to pay

Who was that boy

Waitai piped tunes by an ancient flute
Maiso's zephyred strain a lullaby gentle and sweet
Twittering *toli* a faithful company *em-oot*
Are sure memories of *apek kebile*'s retreat

Who was that boy

His name and memory will forever stand
Ranks with the greatest in the annals of our country
He did us all proud the indigenous of this land
Having knocked out *terra-nullius* and now our land is free

He was that boy

by Eidi Papa (George Mye)

*Dedicated to the memory of a great Torres Strait Islander
Australian, the son of a dinki-di puar amissir-amissir Meriam
of the native title homeland — Mer Island in the Torres Strait*

Contents

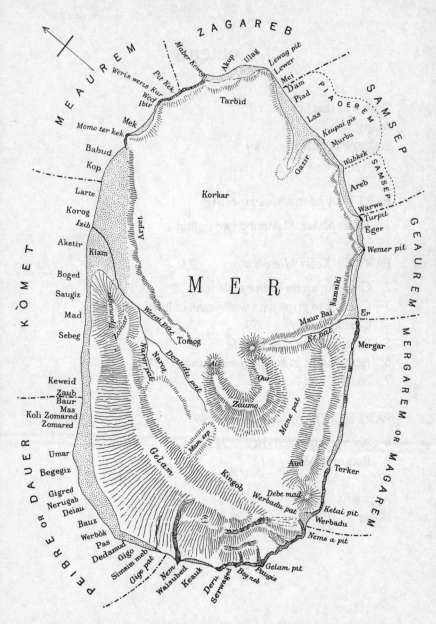

From A.C. Haddon (ed.), *Reports of the Cambridge Expedition to the Torres Strait*, Vol. I, Cambridge University Press, 1908–1935, p. 160.

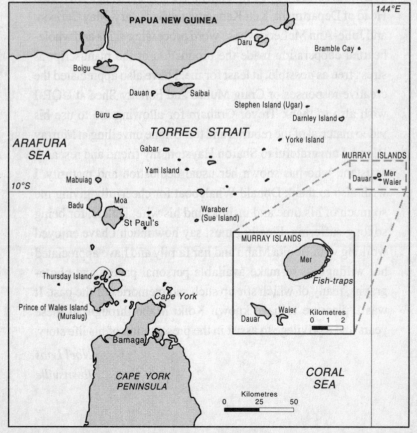

Acknowledgments

I wish to thank Elemo Tapim, Dana Ober, Francis Tapim and Goby Noah for their assistance in helping me understand various aspects of Torres Strait Islander culture, and Anna Shnukal who generously assisted with her knowledge of Torres Strait Islander linguistics and sociolinguistics. Henry Reynolds and I met Koiki Mabo at the same time in 1967 and I have appreciated his interest in this project. Other members of the Department of History and Politics at James Cook University have also been supportive: the Head of Department, Kett Kennedy; the Secretary, May Carlson; and Julie-Ann McLeod whose word processing skills and whole-hearted cooperation made the production of the manuscript as stress free as possible, at least for me. I have also appreciated the creative responses of Craig Munro and Felicity Shea at UQP. I wish also to thank Trevor Graham for allowing me to use his video material of the reburial and tombstone unveiling at Murray Island. I am grateful to Sharon Hayston, my friend and research assistant, who has shown her usual dedication and maturity. I wish also to thank Donald Whaleboat for cheerfully giving me so much of his time and insight, and his wife, Dulcie, for being so long-suffering. Finally I must say how much I have enjoyed working with Bonita Mabo and her family and have appreciated her willingness to make available personal papers and photographs, many of which stir up such sad memories of the past. It was a pleasure to have known Koiki Mabo through all these years and a privilege to assist in the presentation of his life story.

Noel Loos
Townsville

Prologue

When I last saw Koiki Mabo, he was lying in a bed on the lawn in the backyard of his home in Townsville underneath a large canopy which shaded him from the tropical sun. A tent-like net protected him from the mosquitoes and sandflies. He had become tired of being locked up inside the house. My wife and I sat in chairs at his bedside and yarned about old times and the progress of his court case to establish native title to the land claimed by the three surviving Murray Islander litigants. It was January 1992. Koiki hoped this would be the last court case he would have to fight.

Ten years previously the Murray Islanders had begun their battle with the Queensland Government. Koiki, as ever, was supremely optimistic even though his credibility and integrity had been savaged by Justice Moynihan in the hearings completed in 1991 to establish the factual basis of the claims. At the time, Koiki had been so deeply hurt that he could not talk about it when he had met me on the day the judgement was made public. But Koiki bounced back and put Moynihan behind him. Just another white man pontificating about Islanders. Now he was looking forward to going to Canberra in May to be there when, at last, justice was done and white law acknowledged the obvious reality: that the Meriam people had occupied and owned Murray Island according to their own law for countless generations before white colonisation.

The cancer in Koiki's spine had spread to his lungs and throat and he was going to Brisbane for radium treatment, probably for two weeks. He found it extremely difficult to walk or even to sit up in bed. And although he was still as mentally alert as he had always been, he could speak only in a whisper. It did not hurt him to speak, he said, but only a whisper came out. In his fluent English, with his Torres Strait Islander inflection and deep rolling voice, he had achieved an eloquence and an impact which could rouse his supporters or infuriate his enemies. He was aware of the irony of the situation and even joked about it. It would pass and he would soon be back to his old form.

Towards the end of our visit, he raised himself on one elbow and looked at me with the utmost seriousness and confidence, and said: 'Noel, when I come back, we'll finish that story.' 'Right,' I said with an enthusiasm born of previous frustrated attempts, although I wondered how I could get that gentle whisper on tape. A week later, Koiki Mabo was dead. The last words he said, to his wife, Netta,[1] were: 'Land claim'.

I had started recording Koiki's life in November 1984, not long after he and I spent a few days together in Canberra at a meeting of the Australian Institute of Aboriginal Studies, now the Australian Institute of Aboriginal and Torres Strait Islander Studies. I had known him then for seventeen years. He was on one sub-committee, I on another, so we only saw each other at meals; some of these very lengthy and enjoyable ones as we talked well into the night. I realised then that, though we had been close friends for a long time, I really didn't know much about him at all.

I met Koiki in 1967 when we were both on the committee convening the Inter-Racial Seminar held at Townsville in December 1967. It was called 'We the Australians: What Is to Follow the Referendum?'. It was Koiki who had first suggested to Fred Thompson of the Townsville Trades and Labour Council the need for a conference on the status of Aborigines and Islanders in the Australian community. Our friendship dates

from this time. We had been on committees together and participated in various interracial issues that had arisen in the Townsville community, and my wife and I had attended his daughters'
weddings.

When he worked as a gardener at James Cook University we
had frequently run into each other. For a time you could always
find Koiki in his lunch hour, in work clothes, poring over
Haddon's six-volume *Reports of the Cambridge Anthropological Expedition to the Torres Strait*. He was totally unaware of the
incongruity, in those days, of an uneducated black gardener, in
an all-white elitist institution, using his lunch hours to check out
the findings of a group of revered white English academics. Or
if he was aware of it, he didn't care. The journey through his
people's past in this white man's vehicle was too fascinating. He
was also intrigued by these white tourists from another time and
another place.

In 1984 I knew of his political activities and his commitment
to the struggle for social justice. I had seen him at his combative
best involved in various controversies within the black community and knew of his Herculean struggle against a hostile or
uncaring white society to establish and maintain for twelve years
Townsville's Black Community School, the first of its kind in
Australia. We had met and talked together countless times over
the years. I had even had him as a student for a semester in one
of my classes when he had considered becoming a teacher at the
Black Community School. I regularly asked him to address the
students in my race relations course and had learnt a great deal
from him in the formal lectures and in the many informal
contacts we had over the years. But on that weekend in Canberra
I caught glimpses of a life about which I knew almost nothing.
Returning to our motel one night, I said, 'Koiki, we should be
putting this down on tape.' And so, soon after, I began to

interview him, not as the detached academic — that was not possible — but as a friend, a point that is sometimes embarrassingly clear on the tapes.

We always meant to continue recording, but Koiki's ten-year involvement in the struggle for the acknowledgment of native title became ever more intense and more demanding. He was frequently on Mer, or in Melbourne, Canberra or Brisbane. I was often not aware when he was in Townsville. None of this seemed to matter a great deal because we could always get together later. Tragically, that was not to be. After his death his wife, Netta, also asked me to finish 'that story'. I was very much aware of the gaps that I had meant to fill. In 1984 he was interested in recording his early life growing up as a Torres Strait Islander, a Meriam man of the Piadram Clan,[2] under Queensland's oppressive colonialist administration. We also talked about the Black Community School, the positions Koiki had held on committees, and the progress of the claim for native title, but I recorded little or nothing of them. That could come later. Of course it never did.

What, then, I have to offer here are fragments of the life of Koiki Mabo.

When I met Koiki Mabo in 1967 he was 31 years old. He had spent most of the first twenty years of his life on his beloved Murray Island, Mer in his language, Miriam.

The three small islands referred to as the Murray Islands are Mer (2.79 kilometres long and 1.65 kilometres at its greatest breadth), Dauar (1.58 by 0.76 kilometres) and Waier, a horseshoe-shaped, rocky outcrop, the remains of a volcanic crater. The ancient volcanic origin of the islands has left good areas of fertile soil on Mer, which is lushly vegetated, and to a lesser extent on Dauar. Prior to European contact, Mer supported a dense population, with estimates commonly ranging from 500 to 700. Dauar was only intermittently inhabited after the establishment of Queensland control but was very much part of the Meriam domain. Waier was the site of the Waiet cult and its ritual activities but was not inhabited. Almost half the coastline of Mer is fringed by vast, stone-walled fishtraps whose ancient origins are unknown.

Mer is commonly known and referred to as Murray Island, even by the Islanders who, however, use the names interchangeably. It is situated about one kilometre north of Dauar and Waier which are very close together, surrounded by the same fringing reef. The three islands are situated at 10°S latitude and 144°E longitude, the most easterly of the Torres Strait Islands. They have a tropical climate with a dry season and a wet season. Dominating the landscape of Mer is the long steep hill, Gelam, richly enmeshed in myth as is so much of the island. Gelam, in the form of a dugong, brought fertile soil to Mer from the east, and coconuts and yams and other food sources. He brought agricultural practices to Mer as well as the dependence on the sea.

The *agud*, Bomai, a god so sacred his name could not be spoken, eventually resided at Las, which became his cult centre through his nephew, Malo, who followed him. Malo became the outward manifestation of the Malo-Bomai cult, the dominant form of religious expression throughout Mer, and is represented by the octopus, each tentacle corresponding to a Meriam clan and the central body to the strength and unity of Mer. Malo is still respected today and continues to shape the values of many Murray Islanders. Las is in the territory of the Piadram clan, one of the eight clans of Mer. Las was also the village where Koiki Mabo grew up as the adopted son of Benny and Maiga Mabo.

Miriam is a Melanesian language closely related to those of the Kiwai region in the Fly River delta in neighbouring Papua

New Guinea. Mabo believed his ancestors had colonised the Murray Islands from the north-east and could recount a genealogy that went back seventeen generations. He accepted it as the literal truth. It may echo an ancient memory of a population movement so common in the history of the Pacific.

The Meriam lived in the sea and on the land. Their identity, their status, their economic and social life emanated from the land they had inherited. The rich volcanic soil produced luxuriant gardens of taro, yams, bananas, coconuts and fruit trees. Their skill as agriculturalists was valued highly, sanctified by religious ritual to reproduce the productivity known to the ancestors. But there was also an excitement and satisfaction about the sea: whether it involved working the network of rock-walled fish traps, catching crayfish, scooping out silver flashing 'sardines' from a school on to the beach, or setting out in twenty-metre long, dug-out outrigger canoes to catch turtle.

But the Murray Island Koiki Mabo grew up in was no Melanesian arcady. The extension of the Queensland border in 1872 and 1879 to its present extent allowed the colony to control the bêche-de-mer and pearlshell industries that had been developing since the 1860s. Indeed, the Torres Strait was to become the world's most important source of pearlshell which was made mainly into buttons but also into combs and ornaments. The bêche-de-mer industry was less important. Bêche-de-mer, commonly known as trepang or sea-slug, was collected from the shallows without diving suits, and was then cured and exported to China as a food and an aphrodisiac. Japan's invasion of China in 1936 caused the collapse of this industry. After 1912 the trochus industry developed. This shell was also collected by swimming and diving and so provided employment to large numbers of Torres Strait Islanders, including the young Koiki Mabo. When the Japanese were excluded from the pearling industry after the Pacific War, Torres Strait Islanders, mainly from the Western Islands, became divers and skippers, whereas previously they had been only deckhands. Pearls were only ever a profitable sideline in this industry.

Throughout the twentieth century, an oppressive white administration had segregated the Meriam and other Torres Strait Islanders from mainland developments under the policy of protection. It had fostered the change from a comfortable, satisfying subsistence economy to a cash economy based on the fisheries. The coming of Christian missions in 1871 had, in effect, reinforced the cultural changes occurring in the Torres Strait Islands. Increasingly the Islanders made Christianity their own religion. They also incorporated their involvement in the fisheries and their participation in the colonial administration of their islands into their culture.

At the time Mabo was growing up on Mer, the Islanders provided cheap black labour for the hundred or so 'Master Boats' owned by white businessmen. Throughout the Torres Strait some Islander families owned their own smaller luggers, called 'Company Boats'. An early missionary, F.W. Walker, had encouraged Islanders to buy their own boats and the Queensland Government had supported this development when, in 1904, they began applying the same protectionist legislation to the Islanders as they had to the Aborigines. However, the Islanders were forced to sell their catch only to the Queensland administration which paid them a much lower price than was generally available from the commercial buyers. The Master Boats and the Company Boats took most of the younger men away from the islands for much of the year, leaving the women, the children, the old men and those who didn't wish to recruit to attend to church and council matters, to tend the gardens, to fish, to catch crabs, crayfish and birds and to collect oysters and other molluscs.

The colonialist controls had been implemented by the Protector stationed at Thursday Island, the administrative centre, and by a teacher-administrator on each of the inhabited islands. As the controls tightened and the Islanders came to understand their situation, they resented their loss of freedom, especially the government's control over their wages and bankbooks, but also such degrading measures as a nightly curfew.

In 1936 the Islanders on Company Boats stunned their white overlords by going on strike simultaneously throughout the Strait. The Queensland administration had created a unity of purpose among people who had previously been concerned with their own island interests. They had also been drawn together into world-wide capitalism through the fisheries, introduced to a world-wide religion and its Torres Strait wide organisation through the missionaries, and become enmeshed in a Western colonialist administration. The 1936 Maritime Strike was consequently successful because of the wider Torres Strait Islander identity produced by colonialist expansion, as well as being caused by the domination resulting from it.

By 1936, the year Koiki Mabo was born, Torres Strait Creole had developed throughout the Strait as a *lingua franca*, and on some islands had replaced the traditional language, but not on Murray. The Islanders were also becoming familiar with English, the third language of Murray Islanders. Torres Strait Islander English had become a regional dialect, as different from Standard English as Yorkshire or Cornish English.

The strike lasted for four months in the Western Islands, while in the east the Murray Islanders boycotted the government-controlled fisheries until after World War II. Their gardens and the sea could sustain them. Indeed, Murray Islanders are believed to have instigated the strike. They had always been noted for their self-assertive independence and had been dubbed 'the

Irish of the Torres Strait'. Strong leaders emerged to lead their fractious people until another strong leader challenged the old order. On Mer, 'everyone *mamoose*', the Meriam said of themselves, everyone is a chief.[3] Throughout much of the colonial history, strong Meriam leaders had emerged to limit as much as possible the intrusion of Queensland's colonialist controls into Meriam life. On more than one occasion they had defied Queensland authority, the 1936 Maritime Strike being but the best-known example before the Meriam demanded of the Queensland Government, in the High Court of Australia, the return of the native title to their land. Koiki Mabo was born in the year of the Maritime Strike and died in the year the Meriam won their ten-year High Court challenge that destroyed the concept of *terra nullius* on which Australia was founded.

The life and achievements of Edward Koiki Mabo, 1936–1992: an overview

After our return from Canberra in 1984 I asked Koiki Mabo to put his account of his life on tape. This he did, without interruption, for some time. We then developed a dialogue in which I asked him to elaborate on some aspects of his story and, in the process, more of his story unfolded, but it was still very much work in progress when he died. Because of his unique place in Australia's history, I have edited the tapes to express *his* perspective of his life in his own words and minimised, as much as possible, my contribution to the dialogue. In Chapter 8, 'A Very Active Activist', I have tried to reflect the kind of life he led, and his perspective of it, from 1985 until his death, as much as possible in his own words, from his diaries and a selection of his personal papers. This then is Koiki Mabo's perspective of his life. It is my attempt to complete the autobiography we set out to create.

To enable the reader to fit these fragments of Mabo's life into a more coherent whole, I have set down a more comprehensive overview than he and I were able to achieve together. This derives from the material narrated by Mabo, from extensive discussions with his widow, Bonita (Netta) Mabo, and her family, other sources, and the excellent *Guide to the Papers of Edward Koiki Mabo*, prepared by the National Library. There are still uncertainties in a number of areas, for example the duration of the existence of the Black Community School and when he began work as a gardener at James Cook University. With regard to the Black Community School, it seems the written records do not reflect accurately the dates the school operated, probably because there were some periods when the school functioned informally and records were not kept or have not survived. Although Mabo was much more precise than I can be about events in my life, there are times when he may have been a year or so out. However, the overview presented below is as accurate as I could determine, and will be useful for a reader to turn back to, to put some event into a chronological context.

Edward Koiki Mabo was born on Mer on 29 June 1936, the son of Robert and Poipe (sometimes spelt Paipe) Sambo, née Mabo. His mother died shortly after his birth and he was adopted by his uncle, Benny Mabo, and his aunt, Maiga, in accordance with Torres Strait Islander custom. He grew up and went to school on Murray.

Because of his grasp of English, his third language, he was employed briefly as an assistant teacher on Yorke Island by schoolteacher Robert Miles and as an assistant to a Queensland Government health team.

From 1953 to 1957 he worked out of Murray on luggers fishing for trochus shell.

In 1957 he moved to the mainland and until 1960 worked at first on luggers, then as a canecutter, a fettler in the railway, and as a labourer at the Townsville Harbour Board where he found permanent employment from 1962 to 1967.

From 1967 to 1975 he worked as a groundsman and gardener at James Cook University.

In 1960 Mabo had become involved with the trade union movement when he became a union representative and spokesman for Torres Strait Islanders on the Townsville–Mount Isa rail reconstruction project.

In 1967, with trade union support, he initiated and participated in the seminar, 'We the Australians — What Is to Follow the Referendum?', which involved over 300 black and white North Queenslanders.

In 1973 Mabo's request to visit Mer with his family was formally rejected by the Chairman of the Murray Island Council. Earlier requests had apparently been frustrated informally by denying him a berth on the supply boat.

Mabo's involvement in black organisations in Townsville dates from 1962 when he became secretary of the Aboriginal Advancement League, later the Aboriginal and Islander Advancement League, a member of the Australia-wide, multiracial Federal Council for the Advancement of Aborigines and Torres Strait Islanders (FCAATSI).

In 1970, after internal tension, he resigned and became president of the Council for the Rights of Indigenous People, an all-black organisation. This organisation supported the establishment in Townsville of a number of all-black organisations:

the Aboriginal Legal Aid Service, the Aboriginal Medical Service, and the Black Community School.

The Black Community School was the brainchild of Mabo and his friend Burnum Burnum. Mabo was Director of the Black Community School throughout its existence from 1973 to 1985.

Mabo was involved with other black organisations in Townsville and had executive positions in a number. From 1975 to 1980 he was President of the Yumba Meta Housing Association, and from 1986 to 1987 Director of the other Townsville Aboriginal and Islander housing cooperative, ABIS.

From 1987 to 1988 he was Vice-Chairman of Magani Malu Kes, an organisation which stressed Torres Strait Islander identity and autonomy because of what they saw as the neglect of Islanders in indigenous issues in comparison with Aboriginal people.

Mabo's involvement in these organisations made him a national figure in black Australian circles which led to his being asked to be on a number of national advisory bodies.

From 1978 to 1979 he was a member of the Australian Institute of Aboriginal Studies Education Advisory Committee, and in 1984 was co-opted to the Social and Anthropology Committee. That year he was nominated to the History Committee but all committees were disbanded soon after.

At various times Mabo was employed by organisations working directly with Aboriginal and Torres Strait Islander people.

From 1978 to 1981 he was employed as Assistant Vocational Officer in the Commonwealth Employment Service.

In 1985 he was field officer with the Townsville Aboriginal Legal Service, and from 1986 to 1987 he was in a training scheme which involved his being Assistant Director of Aboriginal Arts in Melbourne's Moomba Festival.

From 1987 to 1988 he was employed by the Commonwealth

Department of Aboriginal Affairs as the Community Arts Liaison Officer for the Festival of Pacific Arts, held in Townsville in 1988.

From June 1981 to 1984 Mabo was enrolled in the Aboriginal and Islander Teaching Program (AITEP) at Townsville CAE and, after amalgamation, at James Cook University. He did not complete his Diploma of Teaching but was still considering further tertiary education in the last years of his life.

In 1981, at a land rights conference at James Cook University, a group of Murray Islanders, with Mabo as the leading litigant, decided to take their claim for native title to the High Court of Australia.

In May 1982 *Mabo and Others v. the State of Queensland* commenced.

In October 1982 an unsuccessful attempt was made to reach an agreed statement of facts.

In 1985 the Queensland Government passed the *Coast Islands Declaratory Act* to extinguish retrospectively any native title to land which may have existed prior to British annexation.

In February 1987 the High Court requested the Supreme Court of Queensland to determine the issues of fact in the case. This was adjourned when the validity of the 1985 *Queensland Coast Islands Declaratory Act* was challenged in the High Court.

In December 1988 the High Court declared the 1985 Queensland legislation invalid by a majority of only 4 to 3 on the ground that it was inconsistent with the 1975 Commonwealth *Racial Discrimination Act*.

In November 1989 the Queensland Supreme Court recommenced hearings into the statement of facts. This is now termed the Moynihan Inquiry. Moynihan delivered his judgement on 16 November 1990.

In May 1991 the case was heard in the High Court.

On 3 June 1992, by a majority of 6 to 1, the High Court ruled in favour of Mabo in *Mabo and Others v. the State of Queensland (No.2)(1992)*. This destroyed the legal doctrine of *terra nullius* by which Australia had been colonised.

On 21 January 1992 Edward Koiki Mabo died in Brisbane while being treated for cancer.

On 1 February 1992 Mabo was buried in Townsville in one of the largest funerals seen in that city.

In 1992 Mabo was posthumously awarded a Human Rights Award by the Human Rights Commission and an Australian Achiever Medallion by the National Australia Day Council.

On 26 January 1993 Mabo was posthumously declared the 1992 Australian of the Year by the *Australian* newspaper.

On 13 January 1995 Bob Millington in the *Age* dubbed Mabo one of Australia's 20 most influential historical figures.

On 3 June 1995 Edward Koiki Mabo's tombstone was unveiled in a magnificent Torres Strait Islander ceremony, with Annita Keating present as the Prime Minister's representative. This had been preceded by a celebration of Mabo's achievements in the city heart and followed by a huge feast and Islander dancing at night.

On the same night, the grave was desecrated.

On 18 September 1995 Mabo's body was reburied at his village, Las, on the sacred hill of his ancestors. On the following day the tombstone was again ritually unveiled.

PART I

A personal perspective

1

Koiki Mabo: Mastering two cultures

A personal perspective

Edward Koiki Mabo was a Meriam man from one of the most remote islands in the Torres Strait, Murray Island. He decided early in his life that he had to master the ways of the Whites to exist in the society that the Whites dominated, but never to lose his Islander custom and language. He had a flaring imagination and a determination and courage that enabled him to establish his own community school for his people in Townsville. This courage and determination also enabled him to persist through the ten years of the Meriam High Court challenge. He died of cancer on 21 January 1992, four months before the Murray Island challenge destroyed the concept of *terra nullius*: that Aboriginal and Torres Strait Islander people were too uncivilised to be considered as owners of their own land. This is now commonly referred to as *The Mabo Decision*, or sometimes simply *Mabo*. Through his persistence he and his supporters have opened up the possibility of a new and more promising vision for both black and white Australians.

Koiki Mabo, as he preferred to be known, described the years of childhood and adolescence spent on Murray Island, or Mer, as the happiest days of his life. Indeed, emotionally and intellectually, he never left Mer, even though he lived most of his life on the mainland, chiefly in Townsville. He was banished from Mer for twelve months at the age of fifteen, and actually stayed away for nearly two years. When he returned he stayed for another two years, although employment during this period took him away for a month or six weeks at a time. Even his move to the mainland in 1957 was a typically Torres Strait Island experience, as a member of the Islander crew of a trochus lugger. Between 1957 and 1961, he became a member of the small but growing Torres Strait Islander community of North Queensland and found employment with other Torres Strait Islanders on other luggers, cutting cane, or working in western Queensland on the railway lines. In the jobs he had since 1962, in his creation and administration of the Black Community School from 1973 to 1985, and in the ten-year struggle, from 1982 to 1992, that led to the recognition of native title, he was working in a world dominated as completely by white Australia as was the island he had left as a teenager. And this world was enmeshed in alien codes, values and institutions that seemed, to Torres Strait Islanders, designed to disadvantage and humiliate them and to continue the dependence on white authority they had known in the Islands. Koiki Mabo never accepted white dominance or the inferiority and inferior status colonialist history attempted to impose on his people. Indeed, he maintained an optimistic confidence, sometimes verging on a good-natured arrogance. His absolute faith in the justice of his struggle and the integrity of his own claim was reflected in those last words: 'land claim'.

*   *

The story of how Koiki Mabo became master of two cultures, his own and mainland culture, will seem quite extraordinary to white Australians. Yet in its broad outlines it is typical of those Islanders who have emigrated to the mainland since the end of World War II. This process quickened from the late 1950s with the collapse of the pearlshell and trochus industries after the introduction of plastics.

Koiki grew up on Mer with his own language and culture. Informally, he discovered and learnt his kinship ties and his place in his Piadram Clan.[1] In his village of Las he learnt of the other clans and villages which made up the Meriam people. He grew into the social and economic life of the Island, the gardening and the fishing on the two homes of the Meriam, Mer and the sea. He took part in the dances and ceremonies that punctuated the yearly round or were associated with the rites of passage of birth, marriage and death, especially the tombstone unveilings that the Islanders had developed since the coming of Christianity. These commemorated the death of kinfolk 'Islander fashion', affirmed the ongoing importance of family and friends and celebrated life.

He became part of a devoutly Christian community, itself a part of the Anglican Diocese of Carpentaria whose Cathedral city was Thursday Island, TI to the Islanders. He also became familiar with the traditional belief system, at least those aspects of it that were a living part of Meriam culture, especially the Malo-Bomai cult. It is not clear whether the current respect for Malo-Bomai stemmed in its fullness from pre-Christian times and had been hidden from Western ears until recently, or whether it has assumed greater significance in recent years.[2] I can remember sitting next to Koiki many years ago, certainly before he was involved in the native title case, watching a film that contained very old footage of part of the Malo-Bomai ritual. To my surprise

Koiki was visibly shocked that this part of the ceremony was being shown. It was sacred and secret, he said. In 1984 Koiki discussed gardening and fishing rituals he had learnt as a boy, which he believed were still used. He also discussed love magic and sorcery, *maid* or *pouri pouri* to the Islanders, and various other Meriam beliefs which were current when he was growing up on Mer and which were still so in the 1980s, Koiki believed.

The economic possibilities open to Meriam men in the 1950s were starkly clear. Those who stayed in the Islands could work on the pearlshell and trochus luggers, for less pay than white Australians, or in the few government jobs, such as untrained schoolteacher or storeman, which were also poorly paid. As Koiki approached manhood, opportunities were opening up on the mainland, where Torres Strait Islanders could draw wages equal to white Australians even if in low status, semi-skilled jobs, such as fettling in the railways or canecutting, notorious as hard work under the tropical sun. Koiki Mabo was working on trochus luggers in the dying days of the industry. He visited various ports such as Cairns and saw the opportunities and the different way of life, and it was then that he realised that Torres Strait Islanders were being economically exploited and educated for servitude in the fisheries. The twenty-year-old Meriam man decided 'to give it a go and see what happens'. He set out for the mainland on a great and challenging adventure in an alien land.

A number of factors seem to have contributed to Koiki Mabo's decision to try to make it on the mainland. He had fallen foul of Mer's Islander administration because of a youthful 'mis-demeanour', which had flung him willy-nilly into the lugger work force. He was directed where to work by the Queensland Government administration in the person of Mr Pat Killoran, then the senior Department of Aboriginal and Islander Affairs (DAIA) official at TI. While still an adolescent, he had directly experienced powerlessness before a white colonialist admini-stration and the Islander Council which then functioned as part of that administration. He had become aware that Islanders in the Torres Strait were economically exploited, whether they were Islander owners of Company Boats, or employees on them or the Master Boats owned by commercial interests. His mother, Maiga Mabo, had also urged him to find work on the mainland because she thought working on luggers was a dead end in the changing world in which Koiki was growing up. Moreover, he had seen the world beyond the Islands and there were Islander friends and relatives already living there in employment that offered financial rewards unavailable in Queensland's Torres Strait Island colony. There was also a freedom from colonialist controls. All of these factors contributed to the move to the mainland, a move that was not seen as permanent and certainly not as a rejection of his culture and people.

In telling his life story, however, Koiki placed great emphasis on the vision of Torres Strait Islanders' future given to him by Robert Victor Miles, Bob Miles, the only one of his white schoolteachers he admired: 'a very good teacher and a friend of all the school kids ... He was the one that taught me the most of English language'. Bob Miles learnt the western language, Kala Laga Ya, when he taught on Saibai, and Miriam when he taught on Mer. He was the first of Koiki's white teachers who allowed the children to use their own language; however, he convinced Koiki of the importance of English for Torres Strait Islanders and of understanding mainland culture. Koiki lived with Miles for a time when his mother was ill: 'it was an ideal situation for us to exchange conversation in two languages'. Miles increased his mastery of Miriam from Koiki, and Koiki his mastery of English from Miles. But he learnt more than a new language —

he was introduced to mainland culture. Koiki summarised the importance of this in his reflection on his childhood:

> My lifetime on Murray, I think, was the best time of my life I ever spent; growing up on Murray and having an opportunity to learn both the whiteman way of life from my schoolteacher, Robert Miles, and my traditional heritage as well.

Koiki's English was more fluent and confident than most of the Torres Strait Islanders of his generation. This no doubt was also a factor in his decision to move to the mainland. He was fluent enough to argue with Killoran, to converse with Cairns police and the Commonwealth Employment Service in Townsville and to bargain with the Palm Island administration when one of the luggers he worked on called in there. Because of his command of English, he often found himself the spokesman for his group. In the 1980s he was to be the main interpreter of Mer custom to the lawyers preparing the claim for native title, a role in which he was seen as indispensable.[3] Indeed, throughout his life Koiki played a very valuable role in educating those white Australians he came in contact with, myself not least, as well as people such as historian Henry Reynolds, linguist Larry Cromwell, and the galaxy of lawyers he interacted with over the ten years of the Murray Islanders' struggle.[4] In many ways he repeated the relationship he had experienced with Bob Miles.

In 1959, at the age of 23, Koiki Mabo took a job with a construction gang on the Queensland Railways at Hughenden in western Queensland. This was the beginning of his involvement with the working-class movement: 'I learnt quite a bit about trade unionism while in the railways because of the fellows at the Hughenden Railway Station'. He became a union representative on the Townsville–Mount Isa rail reconstruction project and encouraged other Islanders to join unions. After his marriage in October 1959, he had returned to the west with Bonita (Netta) to earn money for a deposit on a house. Back in Townsville after two years, Koiki returned to his old job as deckhand on the *Lalor* where he worked, all told, for seven years. During this time he became more involved with the trade-union movement, at first informally. At the time, the 1960s, many of the union leaders in Townsville who supported Koiki were members of the Communist Party: Eddie Heilbronn, Bill Timms, Bill Irving and Fred Thompson. In one way this was fortunate as the Communist Party had demonstrated a formal commitment to Aboriginal advancement reaching back to 1931 and affirmed in 1943. This had clearly been accepted at branch level in Townsville.[5] However, in the Queensland of the 1960s, dominated by the National Party, Koiki came to the conclusion that the Harbour Board administration was persecuting him for his political associations by moving him to an unattractive job where his pay was less. So in 1967 he resigned and took a job as a gardener at James Cook University, a job which he held until 1975.

During his time at the Townsville Harbour Board, Koiki had begun to participate in black organisations. In these early years the membership of these organisations was Aboriginal with a few Torres Strait Islander and South Sea Islander exceptions. Koiki became the first secretary of the Aboriginal Advancement League in Townsville which consisted of about nine members of whom five were active in decision making. The Townsville Branch distributed leaflets from the Federal Council of the Advancement League, raised funds, became associated with the Townsville Trades and Labour Council and attended their fortnightly meetings. Koiki and Dick Hoolihan were the Advancement League's regular representatives and, in Koiki's eyes, this relationship with the Trades and Labour Council was very important in his formation as an activist. The union leaders encouraged the black representatives to raise issues but refused to speak on their behalf. Mabo grasped these opportunities to improve his English, to gain confidence in public speaking and to learn to be an activist in a mainland setting. He was a fast learner.

The most important immediate consequence of this was the 1967 Inter-Racial Seminar, 'We the Australians: What Is to Follow the Referendum?', which involved 300 participants, black and white, to discuss the future of race relations in Australia in general and Townsville in particular. This conference was of such historic importance that Professor Charles Rowley referred to it in *The Remote Aborigines*.[6] Following the success of the 1967 referendum, Koiki had suggested to members of the trade-union movement the need for such a conference in order to raise the awareness of all members of the North Queensland community to the problems confronting indigenous Australians.[7] The subsequent organising committee involved members of the black community, including Koiki, as well as representatives from the trade union-movement, James Cook University and the churches. Koiki Mabo's initiative had brought together a coalition of committed people, many of whom were to retain their interest and involvement in the years to follow. Some maintained a kind of Bob Miles relationship with him until his death. Indeed, Mabo once told me that he had realised that there were sympathisers in the union movement and academia who could assist him to master the white Australian world he was encountering, and he deliberately cultivated them.

Mabo considered his understanding of mainland politics was largely derived from his involvement with the trade-union movement, but initially he didn't even know what 'Communism' or 'Communist' meant. Although some attached this label to him, he said he was never tempted to become a member.

He made great use of his link with academia before and after taking employment at James Cook University as a gardener. He was asked regularly to speak to students in my race relations course and also addressed students in other areas such as education. He used the James Cook University Library to discover what had been written about his people, especially in the Haddon Reports, and in the process not only realised that white academics had a lot to learn and often made mistakes, but expanded his own knowledge as he grafted on new insights to his old understanding.[8]

One of the most important insights Mabo obtained, and one which was to have Australia-wide significance, came about by accident. He learnt that he did not have legal title to his land on Murray Island. At some time between 1972 and 1975 Koiki Mabo, Henry Reynolds and I had met in Reynolds' study to have lunch. Mabo told us of his land holdings on Murray Island, and Reynolds and I had the unpleasant responsibility of pointing out to him that the outer Torres Strait Islands were Crown Land; indeed they were designated on a map we had of the area as 'Aboriginal Reserve'. We remember how shocked Koiki was and how determined that no-one would take *his* land away from him. Subsequent events indicate that this was not mere bravado. Mabo also sat in on Reynolds' Australian History lectures and in 1984 participated in my Aboriginal and Islander History course. By this time it was somewhat like having Napoleon sit in on lectures on the fall of the First Republic.[9]

Mabo also attended seminars and conferences he considered relevant, entering confidently into the discussions. At one, the first conference on Aboriginal education held in North Queensland, he was so appalled at the comments being made by some of the teachers present that 'he did his dance'. He exploded into a physical and very vocal demonstration of his Islander identity as a rejection of the patronising and sometimes racist comments being made about Aboriginal and Islander children.[10] As a result of this experience, Koiki Mabo, with his friend Burnum Burnum, established the Black Community School. The school survived for twelve years against the odds and in spite of inadequate funding, active opposition initially from some officers in the Queensland Education Department, and a hostile press campaign in the *Townsville Daily Bulletin*.[11] For some of these years it was the most interesting school in Townsville, with parental and community involvement and the teaching of Torres Strait Islander culture and language. Bonita Mabo, Koiki's wife, who was the fixed centre of his turbulent life, worked as a teacher's aide. There always seemed to be some parents at the school participating in some way in the education of their children.

In order to maintain the existence of the school Mabo was placed in another situation where he had to extend his understanding of white Australian culture. He was Director of the school and President of the Parents' Council, and he had to become executive officer because of the turnover of teachers. The school was subject to a number of reports by white and Aboriginal educationists in order to justify funding. Consequently, Mabo found himself on a rapid learning curve as he interacted with enthusiastic educators such as Anwyl Burfein, Sandra Renew, Geoff Coombs, Rob Renew, Julia Koppe and Margaret, now Senator, Reynolds. Once again he was attending conferences and workshops. He also had to address various groups and approach 'good uncles' (his term) for survival funds. His importance as an educator was recognised when he was invited to be a member of the National Aboriginal Education Committee (NAEC), an advisory body to the Commonwealth Education Department. He appreciated the prestige and honour of being on this body and on the National Aboriginal Arts Board, but he believed that he was the token Torres Strait Islander, the add-on in the title to denote an illusory, indigenous comprehensiveness: Aboriginal *and Torres Strait Islander*. Like many other Islanders, Mabo believed that Torres Strait Islander issues were being swamped by the sheer weight of numbers and political clout of his Aboriginal colleagues who, without malice, simply focused on their own issues.

The Black Identity that Mabo had enthusiastically espoused earlier had begun to splinter into two separate indigenous identities during the 1970s. There was a growing movement among Torres Strait Islander people which culminated in the creation of their own flag in 1992 and their thrust towards a separate autonomy for the Torres Strait Islands. On 1 July 1994, the day on which Torres Strait Islanders celebrate 'The Coming of the Light', the Torres Strait Regional Authority (TSRA) was created as a separate administrative entity aimed at Islander self-management.[12] Some are even demanding 'sovereign independence', a separate nation. In 1994 a candidate for Chairman of Yam Island Council espousing this extreme position polled 50 per cent of the vote against Getano Lui (Jr), longtime Chairman of Yam and Chairman of the combined Islanders' Co-ordinating Council. Getano Lui won the election on the casting vote of the Presiding Officer.[13]

Mabo had advocated a self-governing autonomy for the Torres Strait based on the Norfolk Island model in the early 1970s and had been strongly criticised by other Islanders. In 1976 at a conference on the Border Issue, he advocated 'an autonomous region within the Commonwealth of Australia with its own sovereign rights and the right to secede'. This time the suggestion was received with respect as one that could be considered seriously in a different forum.[14] He was aware of the subsequent thrust for total independence but came to believe that the court action of the Murray Islanders which resulted in native title was the immediate and more important goal. What his position would have been after the 1992 High Court decision and the 1993 Native Title legislation must be conjecture because of his premature death.

There is no doubt that the destruction of *terra nullius* and the acknowledgement of native title has given the Torres Strait Islanders a greater bargaining power with both State and Federal governments, and a greater confidence in controlling their own future and a more insistent assertiveness, the Yam election being just one manifestation of this. Had Koiki Mabo not died of cancer in January 1992, his would certainly have been an important voice in any debate concerning the future of the Torres Strait Islands.

Mabo's understanding of both cultures was very sophisticated indeed in those areas he set out to master. He has taught me and other interested mainlanders a great deal about Meriam culture and history, but freely admitted two things: gaps in knowledge he had never known, and information he had once known but which was now forgotten. His long absence from Mer also sometimes found him out of step with those who had remained behind. They had apparently accepted the Queensland Government's appraisal of him as an urban activist, a troublemaker, a friend of 'reds' and a non-Christian. He said that he had been prevented from returning to Murray on a number of occasions. This could have been done by denying him a berth on the government cargo boat because of an alleged or actual lack of room.

His antipathy to the conservative Bjelke-Petersen Government was blazoned forth in 1973 when the 'border issue' developed as the Commonwealth searched for a redefinition of the border between Australia and Papua New Guinea as that country moved towards nationhood. The Councils of Yorke and Murray both formally refused Mabo permission to visit to record oral history, and he believed the responses were orchestrated by Queensland's Department of Aboriginal and Islander Advancement.[15] When his father, Benny Mabo, was ill in 1974, Mabo was granted permission to visit by the Chairman of the Council only on condition that he did not involve himself with 'political affairs', a precondition he found infuriating and insulting.[16] Mabo believed this decision also resulted from DAIA manipulation of the Councillors. Benny Mabo died on 11 February 1975 before Mabo could make the journey. Mabo's own people were making him pay a very heavy price for the political activism he had learnt on the mainland, which resulted in the confidence and communicating skills which would be so valuable to the lawyers preparing the Murray Island case.

In Townsville in 1981 the Townsville Treaty Committee (of which Mabo and I were co-chairmen) and the James Cook University Students' Union organised a conference, 'Land Rights and the Future of Australian Race Relations'. Koiki Mabo delivered an address, 'Land Rights in the Torres Strait', which clearly spelled out his understanding of land ownership and land inheritance on Murray Island. With this understanding clearly established he repeated and elaborated upon his proposal for an autonomous region for the Torres Strait, within the Commonwealth but separate from Queensland, which would retain Torres Strait Islander customary law. Once again he referred to the Norfolk Island model. Barbara Hocking, then a Melbourne barrister, delivered a paper proposing that an Aboriginal group should consider a High Court challenge and detailed the international and Australian legal history which she believed would support such a claim. She also sketched in many of the major issues that would confront such a legal challenge. The Murray

Islanders returned from a group discussion determined to take up the challenge. Eddie Koiki Mabo became the leading litigant.[17]

Mabo's ten-year involvement with the lawyers and advisers associated with this case led to a sophisticated understanding of its ramifications and of the legal process generally which impressed those who discussed it with him. He was certainly not overawed by what he was involved in and seemed always confident of success. Mabo had been regarded with hostility by members of the white Australian culture on a couple of occasions and rode out the opposition. This was especially the case with regard to the creation of the Black Community School.[18] As a member of black organisations on the mainland he was sometimes a stormy petrel, in conflict with some fellow members and supported by others. Again he seemed to take this in his stride. However, the issue closest to his heart and the one for which he made enormous sacrifices was the one that gave him the most savage and public slap in the face. In his 1990 report to the High Court of Australia to determine the factual basis of the claims made by Mabo and the other two surviving Murray Island claimants, the Reverend David Passi and James Rice, Justice Moynihan of the Supreme Court of Queensland declared Mabo an unreliable witness whom he would not believe in any matter associated with Mabo's own self-interest unless there was other accompanying evidence. Mabo's claims to inherit land on Mer were denied totally. Jeremy Beckett (anthropologist and expert witness called by Mabo's lawyers) has given a balanced response which rejected Moynihan's major conclusions: that Mabo was not the adopted son of Benny and Maiga Mabo; that Mabo's own land claims were invalid; and that Mabo's explanation of Meriam inheritance custom was self-seeking. Beckett pointed out that Mabo's claims were in keeping with Meriam custom.[19]

I can add to Beckett's analysis. I met Koiki Mabo just after his biological father, Robert Sambo, died in 1972. When I expressed my sympathy, he told me he was having difficulty understanding his own reaction because he did not think of Robert Sambo as his father. Benny Mabo was his father. I had already become interested in the process of Torres Strait Islander adoption and consequently the broad outlines of Mabo's response stayed in my mind.

In 1994 Bonita Mabo gave me copies of two letters she had received in 1960 from Koiki Mabo's mother, Maiga Mabo. Both are addressed to Bonita Mabo as 'Dearest Daughter in Law'. In the first, which predates the birth of Koiki and Bonita Mabo's first child, Edward Benjamin Mabo, Maiga Mabo 'roused' on Koiki and Bonita for not writing to her and her husband, Benny. She continued:

> Now you go in the month of Sept. to hospital. I'm so glad to hear this from my head to foot because he [Koiki] is only son for us … If you finish from hospital you tell E.K. Mabo to bring that child and come to home. We wanted look our Grand Child and we want look you too Mrs Mabo.[20]

In the second letter, Maiga Mabo rejoiced because 'our Grandson was born. I'll read your letter for Dad'. The letter is signed 'Your Mum Mabo'.[21] The second letter concludes: 'I am your Mam, Ama [Mother] Mabo'. Neither of these letters was made available to the Moynihan Inquiry.

When Mabo's adoptive status was challenged in Queensland's Supreme Court in 1989, Mabo reflected on two of the allegations that he found offensive. In doing so he demonstrated the complexity of Torres Strait Islander adoption practices. His sister, Marinda Mareko, who was also adopted by Maiga and Benny Mabo, had informed the court that he had not contributed to the cost of Benny Mabo's tombstone on Murray Island.

Mabo's response was that no one had informed him it was being erected so he was not able to. Moreover, he added, his sister had the use of his father's money. Clearly both were focusing on the expectation that he would contribute to Benny Mabo's tombstone because of his status as son. To Marinda, Koiki had always been her brother. At his tombstone unveiling in Townsville on 3 June 1995, Marinda had been accorded the honour of cutting the ribbons to allow entry to the grave site.

The allegation that he had never been happy to be Sambo brought a response that illustrated the gulf between the western concept of adoption and that of the Islanders:

> This is obviously not true at all. I am equally proud of both my biological parents and my adoptive parents as well who were responsible for and [were] designing my future which I am very proud about.[22]

Having studied the Judge's determination and the minutes of evidence of the Inquiry, I can feel some sympathy for Justice Moynihan.[23] He would have needed the wisdom of Solomon and the luxury of hindsight to bring down findings that were beyond dispute. He was requested by the High Court in 1986 to examine the factual basis of the case put by the three surviving litigants. His major conclusion was that a form of native title, a code of custom regarding land ownership and inheritance, had existed prior to European colonisation and was believed by the Islanders to exist still. It was up to the High Court to decide if native title persisted in Australian law after colonisation, that is, after the assertion of British sovereignty.

Indeed the Queensland department administering Aboriginal and Torres Strait Islander affairs had seemed to agree, and confirmed it by negotiating with the Islanders over the use of land, at times compensating them for the loss of their land when it was necessary to build a kindergarten or other public facility, or finding another site if the Meriam owner refused to part with his land. Land disputes were settled according to Islander custom with the Queensland administrator in the Torres Strait (Mr Paddy Killoran from 1947 to 1963), facilitating the exercise of Islander decision making and formally recording the decisions in the court records.

Justice Moynihan had also to proceed to adjudicate on the particular claims of the three surviving litigants, and because of the complexity of Islander custom with regard to inheritance, there were nineteen counter-claims by Meriam relatives to Mabo's thirty-six claims. Seventeen were wholly uncontested; six were wholly contested; and thirteen partly contested, that is part of the land Mabo claimed was contested and a border change requested in these thirteen. Each person asserting ownership of parcels of land seemed genuinely to believe in his or her case and justified it, pointing out how the disputed land had passed from one ancestor to another, going back in some cases over a hundred years to justify a claim. Although genealogies were submitted, much of the evidence was based on oral testimony of how a parent, grandparent or more remote ancestor had said the land was to be distributed. Such claims attempted to take account of direct biological or blood descent, the bewildering frequency of Islander adoption and fostering of closely related children (and the difference these two processes could make to inheritance), the legitimacy (or illegitimacy if not adopted) of the children, and the wishes of the landowner in bestowing his or her land. This could be done by having a written will registered with the Murray Island Council (Benny Mabo had died intestate) or by a 'say', an oral expression of intention to some relative or relatives who would report it as each had understood the intentions of the landowner. And then, of course, boundaries continued to be a great source of dispute as they had been in Melanesian societies before European intrusion. All of these issues were raised in the Supreme Court of Queensland in the dispute over what was or was not land inherited by Koiki Mabo. Needless to say, land disputes are still occurring in the Torres Strait today. In such disputes, past and present, participants claim all of the land they believe they own, regardless of how unreasonable this may seem to the other Islanders in the dispute, whose claims will of course seem equally unreasonable to their opponents. As we shall see in Chapter 8, even on his death-bed Koiki Mabo asserted his claim to the lands that were under dispute in the Moynihan inquiry. I personally found the sincerity of my dying friend convincing and very moving. To date his land claims have not been rejected by the Murray Island Council. Indeed, he is buried at Las on land the ownership of which was under challenge. Many of his claims, however, are not disputed at all.

The High Court gave up the battle to determine which particular claimant owned which particular pieces of land. On 3 June 1992 it declared that, throughout Australia, native title had existed before European colonisation, 'from time immemorial', and that it still existed unless it had been subsequently extinguished by the sovereign state, in this case Queensland, by land legislation that disposed of it freehold, or through leasehold title which was incompatible with the pre-existing native title. The High Court decided that where 'native title' still existed it was up to 'the natives' to determine who owned the land, as indeed Justice Moynihan had recommended in his report. This the Meriam had been doing 'from time immemorial'.

Two-thirds of the Torres Strait Islander people live in mainland Australia, the single largest concentration being in Townsville. Mabo became one of the most prominent members of this community. At some time in the last years of his life he became again a practising Christian. This was obviously very important to him and no doubt was very satisfying to many members of the Torres Strait Islander community which has a very high rate of church affiliation, much higher than in white Australian culture. At the wedding of his daughter, Maleta, on 1 October 1988, the formal speeches were given by pastors from the various Islander churches, each one a mini Christian sermon, at least to these white Australian ears. At one stage I was sitting talking to Koiki when a group of Islanders began singing Islander hymns. Koiki immediately rushed off to join in. I could not help thinking back to the opening of the Iris Clay Aboriginal Hostel in Townsville in 1975. I had been standing alongside Koiki when Canon Boggo Pilot led the hymn singing. Koiki joined in but said in an aside to me that he didn't really believe in it. He joined in the singing because it was Islander custom — like Christmas for white Australians, he said. Now Koiki had moved back into the heart-land of Torres Strait Islander culture, at the same time as Torres Strait Islander culture was moving towards the political and legal positions he had espoused so many years before.[24]

Koiki Mabo determined early in his life to master white Australian culture and to deepen his understanding of his own. As he bridged both cultures, he suffered deep hostility and hurt on a number of occasions but bounced back with his usual resilience and confidence, even after Justice Moynihan's damning personal condemnation of him. At Koiki Mabo's funeral, Bryan Keon-Cohen, the Melbourne lawyer who had worked on the Murray Island case throughout the whole time it was before the court, paid tribute to the man who had led him patiently to an understanding of Meriam law and culture. His deep respect for Koiki Mabo was not merely provoked by the funeral but was clearly evident on other occasions:

I confine myself here to the Land Rights case. The most significant point to make is that without Eddie the case would probably never have begun. As Professor Loos has said, he was truly inspirational. The case began when Eddie gave a speech at a conference here in Townsville in 1981. He spoke of Murray Island customs and traditions concerning land and urged that something should be done to have those customs recognised in Australian law. That speech triggered a very long legal saga that changed the lives of many people. Certainly it changed my life and that of my family and may yet bring even greater reforms and hopefully improvements for the lives of all Murray Islanders ... Throughout this last decade Eddie demonstrated to me many fine qualities which will be well-known to you all. But for me and the lawyers we particularly remember his friendliness and hospitality, his initiative and originality, his courage and quiet determination, his intelligence and astonishing knowledge and memory of his people, his island, its history, customs and traditions. Above all I remember his deep commitment to correcting historical wrongs, some very personal, and to achieving recognition of traditional land rights of his family and his people. He was in the best sense a fighter for equal rights, a rebel, a free-thinker, a restless spirit, a reformer who saw far into the future and far into the past.[25]

The Koiki Mabo I knew was all of these things and certainly saw 'far into the future and far into the past'.

PART II

Koiki Mabo's story

2

Growing up on Murray Island

'The best time of my life'

Koiki Mabo began telling me his life story by singing a song popular throughout the Torres Strait. The first three lines are in Miriam, the language of the eastern Torres Strait. The last six lines are in Kala Laga Ya, the language of the western and central islands. The meaning and sentiment are known to all even though the words in the other language are not.

The JI of the song is Jervis Island (Mabuiag), a western island, but the situation it refers to could apply to every island community. The pearling and trochus shell luggers are leaving the island with many of the young men aboard. The work and adventure are still to come. Now is the sad time of farewell to the beloved island home and the families left behind.

Mabo is singing with a group. Later, he will begin recounting 'that story' at first on his own and then later in a dialogue with me. He is a man of great eloquence, his deep voice reflecting his

natural dignity and self-confidence. Like all Torres Strait Island-
ers he sings as naturally as he talks and breathes, and in this
song he conveys beautifully the sentiment and melancholy of
leaving behind his beloved Murray Island, Mer, kara ged, *my*
home, ina sawth dhawdkay, *for the south land of Australia.*

> Wai JI
> kara ged
> kara ormar barki.
> Ina ngoelmun rangadh
> nangulka kosiya e
> ina sawth dhawdkay
> pogiya dhadh thoerayk e e.
> Ngoey matha gubaw makanu
> tadik sawthaka e
>
> How sad it is JI
> my home
> my sorrow goes out to you.
> We are travelling
> down along a course.
> The south land of Australia
> is covered in fog.
> We are just moving along with the wind
> moving south.[1]

I thought I'd sing a little song first before I start telling my story
because it clears my mind a bit.

I was born on Murray Island in 1936, and I was brought up
by my uncle who then assigned me under his name when I first
went to school. After I realised that I wasn't a Mabo, I didn't
want to change because they were the only people that I knew
in my early life and it was also an advantage for me to grow
under that name because all the rest of my relatives were Sambos

and there were too many of them, and there were too many to share the small bit of land that we had. And my adopted parents told me that it would be better for me to stay because traditionally I became the head of the Mabos. And because of these things that I've learnt to realise the importance of, I then continued to be Mabo. I have no intention of changing my name back to Sambo because of these ideas that have been set in my mind by my parents.

Anyhow, I went to school on Murray and my first school-teacher was Bakoi Baud. She was my infant teacher and she taught me in both Meriam Mir and in English, although her English wasn't as good; but nevertheless she made an attempt to try and teach me to understand the outside world through that language. She taught me to count and we used shells that we collected on the beach. That's how I learnt to count. As I grew up Sam Passi took over then, and my uncle, Meb Salee. Sam Passi was a teacher during the war years and Meb Salee joined him after the war and it was during that time that my uncle, Meb Salee, insisted that we speak English at all times in school, and I used to get into a lot of trouble over that because whatever Bakoi had taught me in the first place wasn't good enough for me to make conversation with others, so it was wrong for them to stop me from talking my language. But that didn't make any difference to me at all, because despite the fact that they used to belt me every time I talked Meriamish, I continued to do so. And nearly every day I used to bend over the table for the old fellow, like Meb Salee, to give me a few straps on my backside.

Anyhow, after Meb Salee, although Meb Salee was still there, we had a white teacher by the name of Mr Cooley. Cooley, regardless of how smart he was, didn't make any difference to my education at all because I didn't understand him and he didn't understand me. And the same went for all the kids that were in the school with me; and the only people that we were able to communicate with were the Island teachers. And he was only there to fill in time, to spend the Commonwealth or State money, whatever it was. After a while Mr Cooley left and we had a fellow by the name of Garlick, although we didn't know his first name. I never ever learnt their first names at all. Maybe in some ways we were forbidden to know his first name. I don't know why, but maybe as a kind of respect. Maybe.

After Mr Garlick, we had a very good teacher and a friend of all the schoolkids. His name was Robert Victor Miles. He came from Victoria. He completed his education degree in Melbourne University and he took a job during the war as an education officer, and then after a while he went up to the Straits and was an education officer of the Torres Strait Light Infantry Battalion. Then after that, he came home to Melbourne, that is, after the war, and applied for a job on TI [Thursday Island]. Of course there were no jobs around the place, so they gave him a job as an administrative officer. I don't know what position he occupied, but he was in the office for a while. Then the vacancy came on Saibai. He went to Saibai and then later he came to Murray.

That was the biggest breakthrough that I have ever had in terms of English language. He was the one that taught me the most of English language. He taught me to make conversation effectively with other people and he was there continuously for me to talk to him; and whenever I made a mistake, of course, he stopped me and then explained the meaning of the word in my language. That was the advantage. He spoke fluent Meriamish. The same thing happened on Saibai. He was a fluent Saibai speaker and he was the first teacher that told us not to stop using our language. And I continued to talk to him. He later asked me why I came to stay at his place when my mother and father went to TI. And I told him that he was the one that requested my stay there, requested me to come and stay. And he wanted to know the reason why I accepted it, and I said, 'Because there was no problem in communicating, and I wanted to practise to talk English language.' And he had me do it. It was a good exercise for him to have somebody, after school hours, to talk Meriam Mir as well, because it was an ideal situation for us, to exchange conversation in two languages; and I think I became the first Meriam man to speak so fluently. Not that I'm very good, but it's better than the majority of my people in that age group.

My lifetime on Murray, I think, was the best time of my life I ever spent, growing up on Murray and having an opportunity to learn both the whiteman way of life from my schoolteacher Robert Miles, and my traditional heritage as well. Now the same thing was also recorded by my mother, and my older brother, Robert, at the age of 17. He was a high school student on Mabuiag when he died, but I've managed to retain the notes that he had written when he was in primary school on Murray, under a white teacher by the name of Frith. I can't remember his other name. There was another guy as well, but anyway he left. He kept some notes. I've also managed to retain my mother's notes as well, and they sort of reflect back and refresh my memory every time I browse through them.

Now when I was born, my dad, Robert Sambo, was a councillor on Murray. He was number two councillor. Marou was the Chairman. Robert Sambo was a very outgoing man and outspoken as well, and he didn't like the attitude of the Meriam people because, for some reason or other, he was dissatisfied because the majority of them would not follow his work pattern, the way he worked on luggers and managed to own boats and so on. And then he withdrew from the luggers and went and joined the army. But before he did, he was one of the leaders involved in the strike action back in 1936, the year I was born. He used to tell me that it was during that time when O'Leary, as a Deputy Director, went to TI with some members of the Master Boats. There were Master Boats and Company Boats. The Master Boats were the ones owned by the European people and Japanese on TI; and Company Boats were owned by Islanders themselves.

Now it's interesting that, at the turn of the century, we became boat owners. We owned boats according to our clan groupings. Say, for instance, my father and his cousin, Kaikai, had a boat themselves (my father Benny I'm talking about, Benny Mabo) and him and his cousin, Kaikai Missi, had a boat; or fathers before that owned the boat, and then, of course, it was handed over to them, and it was during their time that they decided to let the boat go. The boat just remained unattended until it sank. They were in fear that the Native Affairs Department would take the boat away from them if they kept it maintained and in good order. Something like that.

But, anyhow, back in 1936 Robert Sambo and an old fellow by the name of Jacob Gabey, who later went to Kubin as a school teacher and lived there until he died in 1960, I think, or '61, attended a meeting. It was during that time when O'Leary and some of the people from TI, white Master Boat owners, like Hocking, Bowden and all the others, arrived on TI on the *Melbidir* and decided to hold a public meeting in the school building. The school house was made out of tin, just tin with no ceiling and about three feet off the ground, and the hall was packed. The school building itself was about 100 feet long and about 40 feet wide, or 30 feet wide, something like that, and we used to call it the big school house; *au erwer meta* was our Meriam name. Anyway, the meeting was held in there and O'Leary tried to convince them that the conditions that they were offering were much better than the conditions they had before, and, of course, the men didn't like it. And they said all they could see was men jumping through the windows and taking off home. They didn't want to hear any of that rubbish that was being distributed in that room. So, in the end Jacob Gabey and the Chairman, Marou, were the only ones left. Even the second councillor, Robert Sambo, jumped out the window and went home. Didn't want to hear all that rubbish. Anyway, it continued on for a while, and I think Nonie Sharp quotes that in her paper.[2]

It was after that time that Robert Sambo decided to go woodcutting, and I was still a baby. At that time I was handed over, after my mother died, to my uncle, and he then went across and cut wood on the mainland where it was shipped across to the Japanese and a local market on TI. And my dad then, Benny Mabo, didn't have any way of supporting us, so he engaged a boat from his cousin, Captain Oth, and started working on it. And the only reason that he did that was because there were no other jobs around and the IIB [Island Industries Board] store was offering much less price, but it was right here at home. So he, I think, got one and six a pound when the open market on TI was offering something like five shillings a pound. So, anyway, he worked on that boat until he joined the army. Robert Sambo, on the other side, went and was a woodcutter, and my older brother went to Mabuiag, to the secondary school there under Mr Frith; and in 1941 he died at the age of 17 while still at the school.

My biological father, Robert Sambo, was the first Torres Strait Islander to join the Australian army, after negotiating with the officers to find out whether the equal citizenship rights were going to be attained by the ex-servicemen after the war. And, without knowing the politics of the country, he talked with them instead of the politicians. But, anyhow, there was some agreement made, a verbal agreement made by the officers, that all the Islanders were going to get equal rights after the war. And, of course, he joined up and the others followed him.

He became the recruiting officer and they dressed him in full uniform and sent him out to the islands to recruit men. Now it was during that time, I was about four I think, when he turned up. I remember using my first toothbrush and Colgate toothpaste during that time. They dressed him up to impress the others and gave him whatever went on with the army supplies and so on. And I remember wearing his hat and his big boots down the streets of Murray, pretending to be a soldier, without knowing he was my biological dad.

But anyway, the war came. My dad, Benny Mabo, was then the sergeant of the police on Murray and had to leave the police work and join the army.

The Act was very strict at that time and I remember people going to court; couples going to court because a girl was pregnant and being made to marry; being made to marry by the councillors within a certain time. And they thought it was also disgraceful for any woman to be a single mother. The thing that they got across to the Islanders was that they didn't want any second-class citizens to be born out of wedlock; so, therefore, anybody who fell pregnant, or any boy who was responsible for making the woman pregnant, was put into jail and then appeared in court and was made to marry that girl whether they loved each other or not. That was the case.

I remember one morning, early one morning, my mum called me in and covered my head up with a cloth, and oh, not with a cloth, but covered my face with her dress because there was a couple being brought to the jail (we used to live not far from the jail) because they spent a night together. And when they were picked up they were in a very uncivilised situation — naked otherwise. And they were brought in naked, the way they found them in bed; and they brought them into jail. And, of course, the relatives later brought their clothing to them. It was very bad.

And I remember a woman being pregnant too, and my mum was summoned to go and interrogate or to question that woman to determine who the father was. And I remember sitting on my mother's lap on the verandah of the house where the girl lived and she was asked by my mother to tell her who was the father. That was, of course, part of that bitter rule — that bitter law — that was made against unmarried mothers.

During the war years, I remember that ships ran aground between Yorke and Yam Island and, of course, some of the supplies that came off those ships were sent to Murray.

Willy George was a Darnley Islander and he was a skipper on one of the American small ships, coast watchers, and he sailed to Murray and had an engine problem; and he wired in to TI, and they allowed him to anchor off Murray for approximately a month or six weeks until the help arrived and fixed his engine. But it was a good experience for me to see a black man dressed up in an American captain's uniform. And it was so exciting.

During the Coral Sea Battle I remember picking up boxes of food, tinned stuff mainly. The labels were worn off, and we knew exactly what sort of tin would contain a certain stuff; for instance, coffee and biscuits were held in a tin not much bigger than small Sunshine Milk tins — all that kind of stuff. And we had stacks of it. That was good in a way because during the Coral Sea Battle all the cargo vessels, the *Doggi* and *Melbidir* and all the others, were tied up and there was no cargo being delivered to the Islands; and all we lived on was whatever we could grow.

But at the same time all the half castes and white people were evacuated to Cairns, and us natives, the indigenes, were left to fend for ourselves. But, you know, when they returned soon after the war, we again came under the 'dog' Act and it was as restrictive as it was before. They left us to be slaughtered by the Japanese while they ran away and saved their skins. And after the war, of course, they came back and put us back into the 'dog' Act.

Before I left school I went and lived with my schoolteacher Robert Victor Miles for a while because my mother was sick, and we lived about four miles from the school; and Bob had talked with my mum to allow me to stay there. It was closer for me to go to school and, besides, Mum was sickly. Anyway, I stayed with him for about two years; and then, when he got transferred to Yorke, he asked my mum if I could move across to Yorke with him and have a job there as a teacher aide; and I did. For twelve months I worked at Yorke Island school and looked after the little ones — little grade ones and twos for a while. I was only a kid myself at that time. Well, that was my first paid job. Then the second one was as an interpreter. Because of this, because of my involvement and my living in with Bob Miles, I became good at interpreting English into Kriol or Meriam Mir or Kala Laga Ya, the Western Island language. After the malaria epidemic had gone through the Straits while I was on Murray, there were people dying one after the other; the biggest lot of people I've seen die in a very short time was on Murray before I went across to Yorke. And then the Queensland Government sent Doctor McKerris to the Straits to do malaria investigation and I worked with her; as an interpreter, and we went all around the Torres Straits to the southern coast of Papua and then down towards the Gulf area to Kowanyama and Mitchell River and all them places to Weipa; and then around the Cape we came down to Lockhart, to Iron Range, Coen, and then back up towards Bamaga; and then we went to TI. That took us about twelve months to do the research — all the areas that I named took us about twelve months. That was my second paid job.

Then I, of course, went home. And it was then 1953. I went

back home and I spent two years on luggers. In '54 and '55 I was on the luggers working around the Straits where I met some of the people who taught me to make love medicines and stuff like that — didn't teach me to make them but they taught me to use them. The manufacture of that material was withheld from me. They didn't teach me that, but the use of it was taught to me. Now it was taught by Emene Monday. Monday is the descendant of Zoog. Zoog was the second last brother of Zaiar the first.[3] I also experienced the ideas of the thing that they used for singing, where they sing people either to *maid* them (*maid* is a kind of sorcery or *pouri pouri*) or sing females for lovemaking. I've also experienced it, but never ever tried doing it myself. I've never come across anyone who would openly talk about the process of *maid* or *pouri pouri*. That was restricted, and my father, of course, wouldn't talk about it at all. He knew something about it. I don't know just how much, but I believe he knew, but he never ever taught me about it, anything about it.

Before I went away to Yorke and around the Straits, I was also going through a process of traditional education, where a lot of people would come to my parents' home and would talk on several topics. For instance, they knew that my dad was the *Ait*; and even up to now I'm still being looked upon as the *Ait* whether they know it or not, whether they deliberately do that, or it is a kind of unspoken, traditional belief that I am still being looked at in that sort of vision. My people would come and talk to my dad about land disputes and land ownership, who is to marry who, and all that kind of thing. And I learnt quite a bit. I attended my first initiation, a type of initiation to defuse my belief in spirits. It was done by my dad. He took me through a whole lot of things to try and make me realise that white beliefs were not the only ones.[4] We also had value in ours as well; for instance, the secrets of yam plantations and banana growing. He took me into a series of those things; for instance, during planting season my dad and I would sleep by ourselves either out in the open or in an area in a house, in one of the houses where there were no women, where Mum or my sister didn't come in during the day or weren't around. And we'd live in that little house by ourselves, and he used to talk to me — not live in a sense of living on a day to day basis, but we went there to sleep. During the day we lived as a family in a big house in the middle of Las. But at night we would retreat and sleep by ourselves. He would sleep on one side of the fire and I would sleep on the other.

My sister never ever went, or my mother never ever accompanied him to the gardens during the planting season. There was some belief that the women's smell was not a good thing to have round the newly planted gardens. And the other thing was that when he took my mother to the gardens, he was always about thirty, twenty to thirty yards in front of her. It is their belief that they must not sleep with their wives or with a woman during the planting season, because they believed that [if they did] the yams and bananas and all the other crops will never have a good crop. So, therefore, women were not allowed to accompany them even in the gardens and they never allowed themselves to sleep with women. And it was obvious, as well, in their beliefs that whoever's garden didn't produce much, they knew exactly what had happened and they would sort of mock him; and all sorts of things would go on as a result of that and, of course, that made that person feel small and that he wasn't capable. I can't use the exact English word to describe that. They would belittle him somehow.

There were secrets about fishing as well. Fishing is a different sort of game from yam growing and banana plantations. It was also believed that, at a certain time of the year, women were not allowed to go out on the beach because the fish or the turtle may not mate if they see a woman or if the woman appears along the beach. There were some beliefs about mating turtle: say if a man goes out after mating turtles and his woman or his wife was pregnant at home, you could rest assured that he'd come back empty handed; but if someone goes out whose wife is not pregnant, you'd be sure that he'd come back with a catch.

There were some medicines and *zogo mir*, the sacred magic words that go with it, and there were certain rituals that you had to go through before going out to the gardens or to the reefs. Then there were certain rituals also associated with the building of the stone fish traps, and again any men whose wives or girlfriends were pregnant were never allowed to walk anywhere on the seaweed that surrounds the traps. They were not allowed to go anywhere near that. There were some occasions after fish traps were rebuilt when no fish were caught; and they blamed it on someone whose wife was pregnant and walked close to the traps. That was their reason for it.

And I was also taught that traps were owned by individuals, traps that were built many, many generations ago. We don't know who built them, but we know who owns them at this stage. For instance, there are two villages — the village of Las is divided into several sections and there's a fish trap in front of my place and one half of it is owned by myself and the other half is owned by a family of Sagigi. When the time came for us to rebuild the trap, Sagigi would not make a decision unless I was in favour of it, or vice versa. So, therefore, it was a joint effort to rebuild the traps; and with that, of course, goes certain rituals that are associated with it; for instance, you'd have to do it at the right time of the year and eat certain food during that time. And, of course, it was a kind of festivity as well. Everybody was happy and got dressed in the best of their uniforms, and they went around the back of the island and they feasted, and after the trap was built, everybody who was helping to rebuild that trap also received the gifts of fish as a reward. And it's not surprising that the whole family, if they want a lot of fish, would go out and help. Of course, each family would receive not only just one fish but maybe dozens, depending on the amount of fish that was caught, and no one feels that the first catch should be belonging to the owner.

But what comes after that remains the property of the owner and anyone who fishes in that trap or catches fish from that trap would then have to return it to the actual owner; and the owner then would either tell you to take the lot home, or maybe perhaps keep one or two for himself and give you the rest, or vice versa, depending on the attitude of the trap owner. And there are times when some people take it without notifying the owner and when that happens, there's a kind of disturbance or row being created between the owner and the people who harvested the trap without permission.

I was put into jail at one stage on Murray, not actually put into jail but summonsed to appear in court, mainly because someone had complained that they'd seen me with some female and I was under the influence; and they guessed I was drinking methylated spirits, but actually it wasn't methylated spirits. It was my *tuba* — a liquor that we make out of coconut palms. And, of course, I was challenged to court and was charged, because two of the policemen that testified claimed that I was really guilty — and they intimidated the woman who was supposed to appear and give evidence on my behalf. She didn't turn up. So the councillors then ordered me to get off Murray for twelve months, to leave Murray for twelve months and work out of Mer; and I did. And that's when I joined the Bowden's Pearling Company on TI and worked under Noel Baker. Noel was a Darnley man. You know, I worked around Darnley and every now and again we would call in on Murray, and they never made an attempt to keep me off the shore of Murray. As soon as we arrived, after the normal duties were completed, I then found my way to my mum and dad and would spend the rest of the night with them.

When I got caught, when I got sentenced to keep away from Murray for twelve months, my intention was to come down south at that time, but I didn't because I had an argument with Paddy Killoran, who was the Deputy Director then on TI (back in 1956); and under the Act, he threatened to put me on his 'green truck'. People who didn't want to work in certain areas when ordered to by the councillors would go and work on Paddy's green truck and earn no wages at all. That was to beautify the area, a kind of improvement plan that they had with the City Council. And all the men would then work for no wages at all on that truck to cart rubbish or to cut grass and build parks, and all that kind of work. And I refused to work for no wage at all. So he said I should have an option whether to join Noel Baker in Bowden's Pearling Company or work on his truck. So I chose Bowden's Pearling company, and that, of course, was when I became a crew on a boat called *Placid*, which was skippered by Noel Baker. And after that, I decided that I'd come down south and I joined the South Sea Pearling Company and this boat was skippered by Asera Saveka, who died in Cairns not long ago. He was a very tough man. And he was a very good stooge too for the administration of that company, because he didn't make much money out of it and we were only earning £17 a month at that time. While I was at the school, I was earning £5 a month and when I went to the research company, medical research, I was earning something like £8 a month — £8 a month, and all that money was going to my mum because I was able to get my feed. The doctors, Dr McKerris and Dr Mayes, were able to keep me anyway. And all of my money went to my mum. And then on the luggers it was £17 a month, and, of course, part of that went to my mum as an allowance. I think I was paying £10 a month to my mum and I drew £5, my pocket money, and two quid was kept aside for little things, like tobacco that I used — mainly tobacco and cigarette papers. And my clothing, of course, came out of the £5 that I got for myself. Anyhow, I joined Asera Saveka and worked on the *Triton*. From there we worked down south.

First time I landed in Cairns was a big surprise to me. I'd never seen a village so big as Cairns. I got sick at one stage. A stinger got me in the eye (and my right eye is now short-sighted) and they brought me into Cairns. And, of course, they had nowhere to put me. The company was not prepared to pay my board in one of the boarding houses, but instead they took me around to the police station and the police then took me around to the back of the police station. There was a little shed, not much bigger than perhaps 20 feet by about 10 feet, and there were about fifty Aboriginals living there, and they expected me to camp with them. And when I looked around the place I saw there was no place decent enough for a man to sleep; so I went for a walkabout down the street, hoping that I'd come across somebody who knew Cairns that I might talk to to find me a place somewhere else. But anyhow, I was unable that night, the first night. I went back and got me swag out. I didn't part from my island mat and my blanket and my pillow. I still had them with me, and I spread my mat at the back of the garage and I slept, and with me was an Islander. He was a police officer guarding that joint where the Aboriginals were; and that's where we camped. And the next day I went out and found another boat which was tied up with a couple of sick men on board and they used the boat as a place to camp; and I decided to join them and informed the officer in charge of the boat that I worked in to send all my groceries to that boat. And it was much more comfortable there than sleeping in the garage at the back of the police station. I was there for six weeks and then went back to the boat. In that boat, the *Triton*, where I worked, there were seventeen men working for the South Sea Pearling Company, skippered by Asera Saveka.[5]

3

Coming to grips with white-man culture

'A total stranger in a different environment'

Before I started working on the Master Boats I was on *Adiana*, a Company Boat owned by the people of Mer. And then later, for the remaining six months of that year, I worked on the *Adai*. *Adai* was owned by the Maza and Zaro families and I worked for them for a while. And it was during that time that the shell price was at its peak. I think it was something like £1000 per ton, and we were being paid something like £500 per ton. It's little wonder that the Islanders after the war, especially the Murray Islanders, lost interest in working in Company Boats, because the DAIA weren't paying much, and yet they demanded a lot of work to be put into the trochus fishing industry in the Islands; and yet they weren't prepared to pay the top price. Why should Murray Islanders work for less when the top market price was being obtained by Islanders on St Paul's and some other islands, and some Whites on TI? And that was one of the reasons why we became disinterested in the Company Boats.

Now on the Master Boat [owned by non-Islander commercial interests] we didn't actually question the pay; we accepted the fact. We believed that wages were similar throughout Australia — until I landed in Cairns, and I met a couple of the Islanders that told me that they made something like £25 every fortnight on the railway line, while we were making £17 a month on the luggers. And I thought then that we were getting a low wage. The other thing I wanted to find out was whether the white people that worked on these luggers as engineers and compressor drivers and whatever were also getting the same wage; but actually they were getting the same type of wages as was being paid to truck drivers and plant operators in Cairns who drove bulldozers and stuff like that; and then I discovered that labourers in Cairns were earning about £25 every fortnight and we were being paid £17 a month. And I then realised that we were being exploited. So it was my intention not to see the full year through, but rather sort of get off the boat somewhere along the line and find something else.

It took me twelve months to decide [to leave the luggers] because Australia, the mainland, was so strange and there were unfamiliar faces and there was a different language being spoken and I was a total stranger in a different environment. And it was a shock to me.

After twelve months I decided that I'd give it a go and see what happens. And, in the meantime, I'd put away some money, the equivalent of airfares from Cairns to TI; and I'd put that away in my bank account, in my Commonwealth Bank book. That was the first Commonwealth Bank book I have ever operated and it took me a while to understand the bank system — how I could operate my account. And then I put enough money in in case I made a blunder of everything here. I would then fly away to TI with that money. But nevertheless, when we came in to sell shells one evening, I decided to leave then. I signed a piece of paper and gave it to my cousin who was on board the boat then, Mapa Kudub, and gave it to him to give to Paddy Killoran [the senior Queensland Government official then at Thursday Island], authorising him to withdraw my money from my Island Industries Board passbook [and transfer it] to my mother's account. This said, 'Please withdraw all the money from my account, account number such and such, and pay it to my mother's passbook'; and gave her name and of course they knew where she lived; and I gave it to my cousin. And that was the last of it, and I packed my port and made my way to the railway station.

I came to Townsville with £38 maybe £40 — in my passbook and £12 in my pocket and of course no job. I tried and tried to get work in Townsville but I couldn't. There was none around. So I packed my swag and walked along the railway line intending to go back to Cairns. And I walked as far as Rollingstone [about forty kilometres] and then I came across a black man who was working on the rail tracks and I thought I recognised him from a distance. I wasn't quite sure until I went closer and I discovered it was David Sam, one of my Piadram members, one of my tribesmen from Murray. And of course he greeted me with open arms and said, 'Don't go back to Cairns, stay here with me for a few days and we will see if we can get you a job around here.'

That was the only time I remember walking in search of a job. I didn't want to spend any more money on railfares to Rollingstone. You know, even if I did, I wouldn't be able to contact the gangers along the way. It was the best thing to walk.

Anyhow I stayed with him for about a week, and then I thought I was useless. All I did was to cook his tea when he came home. He made his own breakfast and I cooked the tea for him when he came home. And then I decided that I should have a job too. I should go into town and have a look. He gave me a loan of £10, so I came by rail-motor into town [Townsville] and of course got myself on to another lugger, a lugger that was sort of on the tail-end of the pearling industry — the bottom was already falling out — and signed up and sent a telegram to David telling him that I had signed up on the boat and I would see him sometime when the boat came in. So out I went.

It was at that time then, I remember going into Palms [Palm Island, near Townsville] where there was another lugger before us that went in and raided the dormitories where the girls were kept, pulled all the wire mesh from the sides and let all the girls out. They didn't scream, they loved it. We had a bad reputation [laughing]. And five boys, five blokes, got away with five women and took them around to Butler Bay and spent three days with them. I don't know where Butler Bay is. I think on this side, the mainland side of Palms. During that time it was rough weather outside as well, and luggers weren't able to go out. So they camped there for three days and, during that three days, the boys were hiding the girls at Butler Bay. And of course, when we came in after them, they blamed us as well, and we weren't allowed anywhere near the village; and we were very desperate to get some water, and at that time I was the spokesman on that boat because all our guys on the boat were worse in English than I was. They were all Islanders, except the engineer. The captain was an Islander too, Dougie Pitt. So I got off and asked permission of the guard, like a police officer, on the wharf and asked him if I could get ashore and he permitted me.

They sent me off to talk to Bartlam, the superintendent, and when I went in I saw Mr O'Leary [the Director of Native Affairs]. O'Leary was also in that office. Something official must be going on. I'd seen him a couple of times up there, seen him visit Murray when I was growing up. He was Director. He was visiting Palm. And of course, when he came, there were flags flying all over the place on Palm — in the school, in the mission yard, and in front of the administration block, hospital and everywhere.

Murray had a kind of admiration of him, but the rest of them had a similar kind of opinion, like Paddy Killoran, and some kind of mixed feeling. He [Killoran] was a good friend, but a horrible administrator, a horrible set of laws.

Anyway, I walked in there and O'Leary looked at me and he could tell where I came from and he said, 'You're a Meriam.'

I said, 'Yes, Eddie Mabo.'

He said, 'You're Benny's boy.' Knew my father straight off, you know. 'How is he?'

'Oh, I don't know. I left him. I've been on the boat for two or three years now and I don't know how they are.'

Anyway, we had a long conversation, and then he turned around to Bartlam and I requested some rations and some water. Then he said, 'Okay. There will be two police officers on the wharf to meet the boat. You can take it to the store to get your rations, and it'd have to be paid cash. And then for your water, pull your boat alongside the wharf.' And if we couldn't get the lugger into the wharf, we had to send a water drum. I think it was about a hundred-gallon tin to be rowed ashore and filled up and then brought back and emptied into the water tank, pumped into the water tank. Anyway, we did that, and while we're doing that there were police officers there all the time, native police on Palm. Anyway, while we were there, they told me about the dance which was on. We came back on board and then Con [one of the crew of the luggers] asked me if we could go in for the dance tonight. So I hopped in a boat and went back ashore and confronted Bartlam again and he agreed, providing that we didn't come ashore earlier than seven o'clock. 'Seven o'clock you must beach your boats and the policemen will take you to the hall.'

And the other thing was that we knew some Island families, or they knew of us. We knew of Island families on Palm and why shouldn't we be allowed to visit them? My request to Bartlam was in that way. And he agreed that we be allowed. But Torres Strait Islanders had a bad reputation on Palm for wrecking the dormitories and disturbing the girls there. Then he explained and went on to say that several of the women were pregnant because of the disruption they had from the boys on the luggers. Anyway, I promised the superintendent on the captain's behalf that we will keep our boys under control, not that I was very responsible — I was fairly young myself — but I promised him on the captain's behalf and he allowed us.

When we arrived, we were like hungry wolves from the bush. We anchored our boats just in front of the wharf, waiting for seven o'clock to beach them. Seven o'clock when the bell rang we beached our boat; there were about ten policemen in front standing on the inside where we pulled the boats in, black policemen.

And as soon as we pulled our boats on shore, we got guided from there to Barki Sailor's place. Barki Sailor was an old resident on Palm, who was a Murray Islander as well, and we went to his place and visited his family, sat around and had some tea. Barki and his family were very sociable and were pleased to see us. And then that night the girls, his daughters, got ready and we accompanied them to the dance hall. And we were not alone. There were four police officers with us to make sure we didn't detour to the dormitories.

And they took us in to the dance floor. While we were walking across, we saw another group, other policemen and girls from the dormitory coming across. They made sure that we were not going to break across to the other side. So all that night we danced. While we were going on our way to the hall, the girls were being guarded just on the side of us by around eight police officers and there was something like twenty-five girls, twenty-five to thirty girls I would say in that group, and they were guarded by about twelve police officers. When we went into the hall, we were allowed to sit in one corner and the girls in the other; and where the girls were, there was an occasional police officer in between; and on every door and window there was a police officer; and this was to prevent the lugger boys running away with the women from the dormitories. And that went on until midnight, and as soon as the bell rang, a curfew was raised. We were told to leave. And, of course, Barki Sailor went to the sergeant of the police and said, 'Look, these boys are going to have a cup of tea at my place before they leave. Would you allow them another hour before they go back on board?' Of course he did and sent two of his police officers to guard us at Barki Sailor's place.

It was very nice of Barki to do that and we sat around and sang songs. We had an hour while the tea was being prepared. We sang songs and did a few of our things, dances and whatever, and then went on board that night. There were police officers there all the time, even at supper. They did what they were told by the administration, by Bartlam. Anyway, after tea we went back to the boat and I didn't go back to Palm Island until I got a job down at the harbour. Then I used to go across just for a social visit to some people that I'd known, like Asan Sam. *Sam* means 'cassowary'. He is not a relation to David Sam I've talked about. He's a Murray Island man and the other Sam, Asan, is a Darnley man.

This was in 1957. And then in 1958 I took a job with the railways and went out with a construction gang out west and I saw a lot of difference then. I learnt quite a bit about trade unionism while in the railways because of the fellows at the Hughenden railway station. They were very much in favour of trade unions and whatever. And, of course, they taught me quite a few things, and I became very interested in organising the Islander groups to take union membership. And it worked effectively for a while while I was there. Then I believe some men pulled out since I left the railway lines. That was four years later.

Netta and I got married on the 10th October 1959. In '58 I came to the Harbour Board, worked at the Townsville Harbour Board for a while as a deckhand on a tug, *Lalor*. And then I left and went canecutting for a while the same year, and met Bonita, met my wife, during the Christmas holiday of that year. And then we became very fond of each other and then a few months later in October of the following year we got married. After two weeks of holiday, or honeymoon as you call it, around Lucinda and the beach resorts in Ingham, around the Ingham area, we then decided to go out west. We worked out west around the Hughenden area in a little place called Jardine Valley. It was about 12 miles east of Hughenden; and both of us had jobs then. Netta was doing domestic duties and helping the cook, who was our sister-in-law, whatever you may call it, at the station. I was working on the railway line. She fell pregnant with our first son, Eddie, and of course she had to stop work and I sent her into Ingham to have the child there, close to her family, and I stayed out west until Eddie was three months old. Then we took him back out west, took Netta and Eddie back out west. And then two years after, Maria was born. And then soon after Maria's birth, we decided that Eddie was of an age to attend kindergarten and there were no facilities out where we were for Eddie to attend, so we decided to come into Townsville. And from that time we have been here.

We decided to come to Townsville because we had saved enough money for a deposit on a house. And when I did, for the third time I walked into the Harbour Board office and obtained myself the same job that I had before, a deckhand on the *Lalor*, which was the best-paid unskilled work that the Harbour Board could offer. So I accepted it again, and for about seven years after that while I lived in Townsville, I worked on the *Lalor*. The workmates were very good, except the Administration of the place was anti-Black and anti-Communist. And anybody black and commo was on the worst end. So they labelled me as Communist because I was seen by several of the Harbour Board employees listening to an old Communist, a very good friend of mine, Eddie Heilbronn, under the Tree of Knowledge. The Tree of Knowledge was the almond tree between the Post Office and the SGIO building; and that's where the trade unions used to have their public meetings or public address on any political issues. And that's where I was seen several times, and I was labelled Communist and, of course, soon after that I got pushed from one job to the other, and ended up on the sledge gang, swinging sledge hammers and doing heavy manual work for less pay on the wharf itself. So I decided to leave.

So I left them. And it was during that time that I was getting very interested and very active in the Aboriginal organisation, the Aboriginal Advancement League. When we established it, I became the first secretary of that organisation and I remained the secretary for the Advancement League for about eight years after that. When I left the Harbour Board, I went to the University and did some gardening work at James Cook. At James Cook there was only half a library, one Humanities building and a Students Union building. That was about all. Most of the trees that are planted out there, I think I helped to plant them, trees that I see now are quite beautiful. That was some years ago.

My first involvement with Aboriginal organisations in Townsville, was when I became secretary of the Aboriginal Advancement League. Actually the Advancement League in Townsville only consisted of Dick Hoolihan, Tommy Sullivan — there was another old man but I can't remember his name at the moment — Saulo Waia and myself and Mrs Stanley, Mrs Dot Stanley. We were the members — and a fellow by the name of Charlie — can't remember his name. Well, actually we had about nine members but at the meeting we were the only members that would turn up and decide on what to do. And, of course, the only thing we could do, at that time, was to attend trade union meetings fortnightly and to hold dances fortnightly and to distribute leaflets published by the Federal Council. We would go leafleting around the city where Blacks lived to give them some idea of what was going on in the Aboriginal Affairs; and nobody was interested in working in that field at all except those nine people. And fortnightly we ran dances to raise funds for our annual National Conference that would enable our delegates to get down to the National Conference in Canberra. And we did that very effectively. In any one year we would raise something like £2000 and that was enough to send several delegates. This continued for a while and then, after the [Whitlam] Labor Government went into power, we then decided to change the title of the Advancement League to Council for Aboriginal Rights. We received our first grant for £3000 and we employed a young girl to work with us; and then after that we received several other grants and we increased our staff to two people. And it was a fairly quiet organisation, until some of my colleagues thought that it was not necessary for Islanders to be involved in Aboriginal Affairs and ran a campaign against me; and at the public meeting that was held, the Annual General Meeting, I got eliminated and that was the end of it. Soon as I pulled out they weren't able to keep the Aboriginal Rights Council going and they also let it flop.

I then went on to be interested in Tranby College and all the other organisations down south and I was appointed as an agent to recruit students for them [Tranby]. In those days there was no such thing as the Study Grant so we continued to run our dances and out of that money we'd send our students where they wanted to go and study in Sydney; and that money would support them. And we did that; and the popularity of the fortnightly dances had increased and that was something like £3000 collected in a year for all the dances. Some of it used to go to the Federal Council and some of it used to go to Tranby College to support the students that were there.

I myself spent six months in Sydney learning about cooperatives, about credit unions. It was a non-assessable course and I enjoyed it and I learnt quite a bit from it. In fact that sort of motivated me to — that sort of made me become more interested in running our affairs. And after a while the dances flopped because there were too many people wanting to get their cut out of it. Like the people who were renting the hall to us, they tripled their price for the night; and the band wanted more money; and of course we ended up losing money; and then after a few more months that we attempted to try and cover that loss, we ended up dropping the dances as well.

It was during that time that the idea of the Black Community School was well under way. It was 1972. And in 1973 we established our own school; and from there I became the first Chairman and the Director of the school and I have continued in that position for 12 years.[1] That was an experience on its own.

That idea of the Black Community School came to me when I was sixteen. I was sixteen years old and I often thought about it, because my mother always talked to me about doing well in school so that there will be a better job at the end.

I learnt when I came to TI that there were kids there that spoke fluent English and I wasn't able to do so. So I thought, if that school was being run by my parents, I am sure they would go to their extremes to find a right teacher and right equipment to be used in school to educate me. The independent school idea hit me then. Why not? And it lived in me for 18 to 20 years before it really came into being. So it wasn't new to me. It was built on, a bit at a time, from there until I really got it off the ground with the help of a friend called Harry Penrith [now known as Burnum Burnum][2]. He put it all together. During that time, from the onset of the Black Community School, I found that I didn't know enough to be able to do it effectively and I stood back for a long time, for about twelve months or more, trying to figure out which way I would fit in, until I was forced to decide when the Principal decided to resign. So to keep it going I just had to play a more active role in the decision-making processes in the school; and of course teachers came and went; and I had no idea, no theory of white education, didn't know the process which the teachers go through and didn't know how and what areas I should look for in terms of selecting the right people to work in the school. With the assistance of some people around the education circles, Margaret Reynolds, Henry [Reynolds], Noel Loos and several others, Julie Koppe and Geoff Coombs, they were able to get me to take certain actions whenever things became necessary.

But I kind of feel now that if the school was to come into existence again, it would be a totally new school. Not that I am very good at it, but I think I have learnt quite a few tricks since that time, because I feel a lot of the material being taught at the Colleges is not relevant. They definitely are not relevant to us at all and the teachers that are being selected to teach in those schools have no understanding of how Aboriginals and Islanders behave, and what excites them and what does not excite them. So in that sense I would be more careful in selecting teachers and perhaps do a bit more in terms of convincing some people about the relevance of the courses being taught, and the relevance of the courses to Aboriginals and Islanders.

For instance, I am being continuously told that the language that the kids bring from home should be the language that they should be taught in. It is a language that they understand. But it is rather unfortunate to hear in our case that we have to employ so-called qualified people to teach us in *their* language. It is a language that we do not speak at home at all. They may be qualified to some people but I am definitely sure that they are not qualified to teach us, because personally they've got to communicate. I have made several enquiries about teachers who taught in the Islands. I'm of an opinion that they were just wasting their time up there; mainly because they were not effective and they were not communicating with the people that they were trying to teach. The best communicators were the ones that were the Islanders themselves. So, therefore, I would think that courses in Island language, how to teach Island language, to read and write in the first few years of school life, would be most appropriate and then English can be taught as a second language. And, of course, there is a fear perhaps in the white academic circles about who you would get to teach. Or perhaps the administrators of the Education Department are in constant fear that they would lose control. It is a matter of controlling the school.

But the argument today that we have come up with is that although they may own the schools, they don't own the kids. Their physical and intellectual development are the parents' responsibilities; so therefore, if the parents decide to withdraw their kids from schools such as the ones they are running now, I do not think that the parents should be blamed for such actions at all. It should be the Education Department who should cop the blame themselves. Maybe, perhaps one day, this sort of action may become necessary. I am not sure, but let's hope that they do realise the importance of that pretty soon.

Ten years after he and Burnum Burnum established the Black Community School, Mabo was asked to comment on a proposal to establish the Brisbane Independent School. He discussed the relationship between culture and family, clan, island, Torres Strait Island, and Australian identities and stressed the importance of community in his philosophy of education — all without any hint of jargon or the echo of a textbook.

From June 1981 to 1984, Mabo enrolled in a Diploma of Teaching course. Although he found classroom teaching in practising schools a bleak and disconcerting experience and did not complete the course, he clearly profited from this exposure to the Western perspective of education and realised even more clearly that it was fundamentally destructive of Torres Strait Islander people and their culture.

After reading the introduction of the report on the Brisbane Independent School, I'm beginning to think that the problem and the basic philosophy is much the same, although I don't know whether at this stage that I should be making comparisons; but one cannot get away from it because of the fact that I had ten years' involvement in the Black Community School and therefore I have no alternative but to compare the two schools. For instance, the basic philosophy of the Brisbane Independent School is much the same as the BCS: the underlying management of the school would be the parents' responsibility. The curriculum development and the whole run of the school is the parents' responsibility. After all, the children we [teachers in mainstream schools] play around with, or we tend to dominate in schools, in public schools, are not totally *our* children. Well, they're definitely not our children. We're taking away the responsibility of the parents and giving it to some alien body and that's one of the reasons we thought that independent schools are much better off than state schools. Besides, education is a parent's responsibility. It should not be manipulated by a foreign body. In the case of minority groups such as ourselves, we're being forced to accept alien culture. One may argue that we need to survive as a race as Australians, but again the actual thing is that the kids are themselves first, before they are Australians. The family units are themselves first. For instance, myself I am a Piadram first and secondly I am a Murray Islander and then a Torres Strait Islander and then an Australian afterwards. Therefore, I need to strengthen my kids with their own heritage before they could accept the overall society's values. And in terms of parents who make decisions in an attempt to educate the kids away from mainstream that is very admirable. There are other things such as the community in which the school operates. In our case, I continuously argued in terms of 'community'. What is 'community'? In my evaluation of the word, it means especially in a situation where the people involved are very closely knitted and have common values and common pride and everything that goes with it; the community in my sense refers to people who are involved in whatever they're attempting to do or whatever they're doing. In a community school such as ours, our community relates to fifteen families whose children are enrolled. Lots of criticisms have been made about community participation in school. Now I don't really agree with having to involve the whole of the community in terms of members who are in it, members that are living in an area such as Townsville. I do not agree, because only people with interests in that kind of area can participate and then they become members of that community. Anyone else who lives within that community, within the urban sense of centres like Townsville, cannot call themselves members of the Black Community School because they are not participants of the school, and the same goes for the Brisbane School.[3]

Back in 1972 I got appointed by the minister to serve on the Aboriginal Arts Board for a while to represent Torres Strait Islanders. It was great in a sense to have the privilege, and of course it gave me status to be on the national committee; but at the same time I felt that I was only a label because Torres Strait Islanders didn't get much out of that, despite my attempt to present applications to the Board for approval; but again it fell in a deaf ear every time, because the Aboriginal culture was seen as being much more important than the Torres Strait culture. And the times and times again that I went out of my way to request people to present their applications for approval of the Board. And of course had negative results.

Mabo clearly believed that the attention given to Torres Strait Islander concerns was at best superficial window-dressing and at worst hypocritical and destructive.

I got appointed to the Education Committee for several years, and of course the same thing's happening in there. With regard to Aboriginal and Islander Education in the Queensland Department of Education, it seems that we are only a label and very little effort is made to change the system so that it would better suit the Islanders and the Aboriginal people. Maybe the Aboriginals in the urban scene haven't got that [their culture] any more. They have lost it. That's their blue; but I hope that they don't bring that on to the Torres Straits as well because we still hang on to what we have got culturally. And the Education Department should be able to make things much better for us in a way that would continue turning the wheels of learning processes for young people, instead of stopping them in the middle of the learning process and teaching them a totally different language. In my opinion we end up as an intellectual ruin rather than anything else. Because the way things are at the moment, that's all we have been.

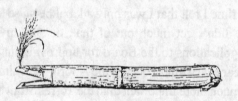

4

Changing ways

'The place is far removed from our sacred traditional area'

I can't remember how Waiet was blended into the cult. All I could remember, it became the actual story of a person coming from the Western Islands and landing on Waier and he got accepted into the community there. But I don't know exactly how the cult started. All I know is that it became part of the Malo-Bomai cult and was a shrine for fertility and there were some rude things that it was believed that he'd done as well. For instance, it was believed that menstruation periods, menstrual periods of women, were caused by Waiet. Every month they would bleed and it was thought that Waiet was the cause of that, and there were some ceremonies held; and I believe, according to the stories that I got from my grandfather, that young girls, not very often, but I think it was once in a while, that young girls were taken and sacrificed [given to Waiet]. They were actual human sacrifices for him.

Koiki knew very little about Waiet, probably because the cult was no longer a living part of Torres Strait Islander culture when he grew up. He discussed the relative importance of Malo, Bomai and Waiet.

Malo was the important one. He was the kind of overall *agud*. *Agud* means supreme being. We call it *agud* [owgood] in the Eastern Islands and *augud* [owgod] in the Western Islands. When the first missionaries went there, the people would say, 'Ooh, ow god'. The first missionaries thought, 'Oh, they already know God' because they're saying, 'Oh God!'

Waiet fitted in as a kind of religion that created a lot of fruit and a lot of people, birth rates and all that kind of stuff; increase the birth rates. I think [the Waiet] cult mainly had sex connotations.

Koiki had seen rituals associated with agriculture, fishing and the building of fish traps being practised on Mer.

For instance, the fish trap ritual: it was practised by the owners of the trap in consultation with the *zogo le*. *Zogo le* means the sacred people, the *Ait* and the people associated with Malo and Bomai. All these rituals — the fishing ritual, well, they still practise it today. But the only method that ceased is the consultation business. They don't go to Las anymore. Las is the centre of the land I'm claiming in court. That is my heritage. It's a village. It was a centre of the *agudism*. It was a very important village in the history of Torres Straits. It would be about eight families; I mean you're looking at about 200 people that are associated with that particular village. Still there. It's on the northern side of Murray. The *zogo le* lived there.

Murray Islanders do not consult the zogo le *any more (the three holy leaders who wore the Malo-Bomai masks), but Koiki was sure they still used rituals associated with agriculture, fishing and constructing fish traps.*

Oh, yes. They still do that. The beliefs of how it has to be done is still carried out, and going hunting. The rituals are still done regardless of the Christian influence; still carried on. Yes.

Murray Islanders do not use these rituals in Townsville when they go out fishing or put out fish traps.

The place is far removed from our sacred traditional area. People don't worry about it. However, if they went back to the Islands, they would still do exactly the same thing.

Mabo laughed gently as he elaborated upon this.

Maybe, you know, the Christian leaders would say that it's a good thing that they wiped them [the rituals] out completely from their traditional areas so that they won't practise the pagan religion anymore. But it still happens. I still see it as a religious practice. People who go to church every Sunday and receive communion three times a week, on Murray. They still practise it. They still go back to their gardens and to the fish traps and go out hunting using the same rituals. People who go to church and read the Bible, the readers of the church and whatever, they will practise it.

I asked Mabo if the Torres Strait Island Anglican priests used these traditional rituals. He said they did, and that they felt there was no conflict between their Christian faith and their old practices. To them it was Islander, 'a smooth blending of both'. I asked Koiki if his father practised these rituals.

Oh, yes. He did that because, one thing, he believed that these practices, these rituals, were beneficial to us, and our trap would get a lot of fish, and we'd have fish whenever we needed, whenever we wanted; just go out to the trap and get it, and come back, you know. And there was a crayfish magic as well. There was a certain way you'd treat the cray, and you do the magic before you set the trap; and you'd end up with lots of crays. They're there all the time. All you do is just go and take out two or three, just enough to eat for supper; and then they'll be there for the next day, and you go out and get some more.

The shell of the cray was placed under the tree where we lived at Las and [we] would sing. There are sacred songs that are associated with it. I don't know the song. That's one of the things that I forgot; you know, I heard him actually sing it, but I tried to remember it when I started recording for this. I just couldn't. I sang these songs when I was young, yes, and over the years. Maybe it will come back to me.

Koiki was conscious of a part of his culture that had slipped away but which perhaps could be retrieved. Perhaps. I asked if anyone in the Islands still sang those songs.

I think so. Yes, I think the elderly people still do.

And the younger ones coming along?

No, They're too taken up with cassettes and radios.

According to Koiki, the Christian religion might not have destroyed all the old Torres Strait Island beliefs, but modern culture, western materialism, was doing so. I asked Koiki why he believed this was happening.

Because of mass migration and exposure to the outside world. It's gradually diminishing the traditional village. That's the main thing, I think. Not the Christian church. It's an exposure to modern technology and modern science [and modern education]. There are some things which they still practise, things that are effective, like poisoning fish. Before, it was believed to have been a magic, but now people believe it's a chemistry, that if you add certain things to salt water, it affects the fish, and they come up to the top and you just go around and pick them up.

Once again we turned to the young. I asked if they believed in the old magic. Some did, Koiki said, some didn't. Did they believe in pouri pouri, *malevolent magic, what whites called black magic?*

Yes, I think so. I think there is a belief still, currently, you know, being practised among the Islanders, yes. [*In the Islands and in Townsville as well?*] Yes, so I believe.

I heard a lot of people talk about it. You know, when someone dies, according to us it's not natural for someone to die. It must be because of something, caused by someone.

They sort of look for signs. There are certain signs that they believe are only caused by *pouri-pouri*. See, another strange thing is that — you know, maybe we're still digesting the fact that your heart can stop beating and you collapse. Right. Whereas, traditionally, back home there was no such thing as heart attacks. People got sick and died. There was no sudden death or someone dropping dead in the middle of the street; these are quite strange to us, and they believe these can only be caused by *pouri-pouri*.

Q: *And what is the reaction in Townsville to someone who drops dead?*

Oh, they will put it down as *pouri-pouri*. (*Some Meriam later would believe Koiki's own death, at such an early age, was the result of* pouri pouri.)

Q: *And who would they see as practising the* pouri pouri?

Oh, there are several people here that they think are — because they are descendants of the people that *their* parents believe were practising *pouri-pouri* back home; and they are being accused of using *pouri-pouri* in Townsville.

I asked if people were frightened of these Islanders, if they had friends.

Well, I've actually approached them and said, 'Look, I've heard people talking about you using *pouri-pouri*.' And they've just laughed and told me they don't use it. You know, the same question came up when I asked Maureen Fuary.[1] I said to her one day, 'You know, if you believe in this *pouri-pouri* man, have you ever spoken to the *pouri-pouri* man? Because they [the *pouri pouri* men] were obviously frightened that someone else was a *pouri pouri* man.'. And the same thing's happening here. The one's that I've spoken to were frightened of someone else.

Koiki considered the belief in pouri pouri *was circular or self-fulfilling. People who were believed to be* pouri pouri *men were feared but they in turn feared other people they believed to be* pouri pouri *men. In fact none of them may have been* pouri pouri *men but they were blamed for misfortunes and thus their reputation grew. I asked Koiki if he believed anyone in Townsville used* pouri-pouri.[2]

I don't think so. No, I don't think anybody's using it. But I do know people still use love magic.

He smiled and then burst out laughing. He was one who had used love magic. He thought Torres Strait Islanders in Townsville also used dance magic.

Dance magic is — you know, when there is a competition

between two groups of people, if your magic is much more powerful than mine, it would make the dancers lose interest in dance, make them sore. Say, one performance and that's it — they're exhausted; and they'll soon go and leave the field for you to perform all night. I know they still do that here in Townsville — especially when there is a big feast on.

Again he laughed appreciatively, as if relishing the thought of his participation in the feast and the dancing. I asked him how else magic was used in Townsville.

Oh competition, well, competition for best garden produce, especially the people that garden around the back yards. They still do that, they still compare and probably use garden magic. I don't know because someone hasn't told me that they do; but I've got it in the back of my mind that they still do it, from what I know of back home. Anywhere you go in the Islanders' homes [on the mainland], the backyards are filled with yams, bananas, sweet potatoes. I garden at home. At the moment I pulled out all my banana plants. My kids complained there was no room there for them to run around so I had to pull them all out.

We both laughed at the familiar situation of a father under seige.

I've [also] brought several trees from the Islands, fruit trees, and grew them. Nowhere else in Townsville grows them. Actually, I've been thinking of bringing some out here to the university so that Islanders in future could come down here and enjoy them; here in the garden around the university campus.

There is now a native Bell Fruit tree growing in front of the Mabo home in Townsville and one at the back which become covered with bright red fruit. They seem to have relatively little taste at first but gradually become very pleasant to eat. The Meriam call it ero *(pronounced air-roar). There is a thriving patch of yams growing in the university initially planted by Koiki.*

Koiki described the sharing of fish in accordance with Islander tradition.

It depends on where the fish is caught. For instance, if they were caught in a fish trap that would mean that the owners of the trap would be the ones to order which people were going to get a share of that fish; particularly at the time when the traps are first reconstructed; then the fish is shared amongst the ones that help to reconstruct the stone fences. The other thing is that when a fish is caught in an area or on a home reef belonging to certain clansmen, the clan leader has a responsibility of sharing that fish to his clan's members. It still happens in the Torres Strait.

I went back just before I came here to James Cook University. It was about four years ago now. One of the people not far from my clan area called for reconstruction of his trap, and everybody went across there, went around. It's a festival on its own, you know; people dress up in flash clothing. Then, when the tide went out, we all walked out to the reef; and even if you just pick up one or two stones and put them on to the wall your name goes down on the list; on the list of names that are kept.

Before, it was kept in the mind, but now, since we knew the art of writing people's names, we keep a list; and then when the first lot of fish is collected, you get your share of it; and sometimes more than the work you did. The first catch is usually shared amongst people that helped to reconstruct the fences, and then the catches that follow are only shared between the clan members. Or sometimes, if they have a friend in neighbouring clans, well they also get a share as well.

Q: *In the Islands, do the young children join in?*

Oh yes. Everybody does, even the very young ones. Kids from primary school, grade ones, they get out and help, and they get their share of fish as well.

The communal activity and sharing associated with the construction of fish traps was not practised in Townsville. Yet even in the 'strange environment' of Townsville the Islanders shared the expenses of fishing expeditions, weddings and funerals.

No, because, it's a strange environment, I think, nobody does things like that. In fishing, that's the only thing that we've brought down here, everybody shares the cost of whatever the fish may be; for instance, a wedding. That's the only thing that we share, or funeral expenses. Everybody, all the relatives, get together and pay for the funeral expenses.

Koiki referred back to the time he was charged for being with a woman on Murray Island and being under the influence of alcohol. He elaborated on the story. He admitted he had drunk methylated spirits as well as the illegal local alcohol made out of coconut juice.

Yes, I think it was the frustration that led me to do that. I was fifteen I think, or sixteen. No, sixteen. Yes, I was sixteen. What had happened was because of that restrictive rule that you can't talk to people of an opposite sex.

You know, when we talked about it yesterday, when I went home, I thought about it; but it was actually the traditional rule that [for] adultery, the punishment was death for both male and female, in the traditional time. And when the missionaries came, they took that into account. You mentioned before [in a lecture], they were the rulers themselves. They were little governors of the place; and of course, when they did take that into account, they did away with the death penalties and imposed the jail term of anything up to three months.

Q: *The missionaries even stopped adulterers from coming to church?*

Oh yes. They barred them from church unless there was a confession before you came to church. Anyway the same thing happened — when they did that the council adopted it and made it a rule, and it was then supported. Because the council adopted it, the DNA, the Native Affairs Department, took it in as a by-law.

Consequently, adultery was a criminal offence in the eyes of the Queensland Department of Native Affairs.

After, there was a whole group of us who embarked on drinking. I used to make some *tuba* and sell it. *Tuba* is a liquor made out of coconut and I made it. My father showed me that, to make it, and I did. And then one weekend, I don't know what happened, but we all got stuck into this *tuba*, and then we ran out of *tuba*, and someone offered methylated spirits and we got stuck into it [laughing]. Anyway, we got caught that weekend and ended in jail; and I was in there for about a week before I appeared in the court and was charged with both being with this woman and being drunk on a reserve. And then the penalty was that I was given twelve months away from Murray; exiled for twelve months. The Torres Strait Island Council did it, and it was backed by the Department, by Paddy Killoran.

I remember when I came into TI, there was a long line of young people, young men waiting to sign the shipping articles. When I came in to sign up for the luggers that worked towards Cairns, Paddy's native police came around and bailed me up and took me around to him, and he asked me why did I want to come south. I explained it's just that I wanted to go.

He said to me, 'You know you've been exiled and you have to stay away from Murray for twelve months.' And I said, 'Yes, and that's why I'm going south.' And then he said, 'No, you're not going south, you're going to work on the luggers that operate in Torres Strait alone.'

And he said, 'If you don't do that, the alternative is that I'd put you on my green truck for twelve months and you'd get no wages at all.' Probably frightened the hell out of me.

Well it did, anyway, and I agreed at the end that it's better to work for wages than no wage at all. So I worked on the lugger for the first year. And then after that I spent a couple more years before I made my way down here.

Koiki was sixteen at the time. He had not drunk this heady mixture before, tuba and methylated spirits, and was a little embarrassed about the methylated spirits.

Oh, I don't know what made me do it. Maybe peer pressure in a way because the rest of the fellows ... There were some men that were with us who were ex-servicemen, and they knew that from the army; so, you know, when I saw them drunk, I sort of got influenced as well.

There were about four of us. Two went to one of the boats that were operated by Mill Brothers from Nagir; and one of them died while he was diving; and there was me and someone else that got sent to this boat operated by Bowden Pearling Company, and we worked under Noel Baker. He was a Darnley guy. He was a skipper on that boat. We worked for twelve months and then decided to go back to Murray. Then we stayed on Murray and worked on our Company Boats for about two years afterwards, I think. Yes. *Adiana* and *Adai* were the luggers that we were on.

The whole Island owned *Adiana*, and *Adai* was owned by Zaros and Mazas. There, old Mataika Maza was in charge of it and all his brothers-in-law. The Zaro family were the shareholders.

Master Boats were the ones that actually paid wage[s] and the wage at that time, when I started work, was £15, and then it later went to £17.

They were owned by white pearling companies on TI, like Hocking Pearling Company. There was the South Sea, Bowden's Pearling Company and Shipway's. There were several others; and they owned quite a few.

They [the Company Boats] got paid according to the catch, and, of course, the rules were imposed earlier on, before the war I think, that all the Island catches would have to be sold through the IIB, and that, of course, reduced the price. Even at that time nobody was making too much effort to catch too much shell.

The Island Industries Board [IIB] offered a very low price to the Islanders, much lower than was obtained on the open market through Burns Philp. The Company Boats, even though owned by the Islanders, were controlled by the Queensland Department of Native Affairs, especially through their control of the market.

And all the buyers on TI were informed that it was a penalty, or it was a crime of some sort, to purchase shells from the natives.

Koiki explained the paternalist rationale behind the Queensland Government's policy.

I think their idea was that even if the world market for the pearl and trochus went down, the DNA would still maintain that low price. That was the idea so that Islanders would continue to work. They would sell it at the market price to Burns Philp or through their outlets in Hong Kong, [and keep the surplus] for a rainy day.

But the thing was that, even in previous times, Torres Strait

Islanders never starved, because they were in the home grounds. They know exactly what to grow at what time of the year, so it can be productive in a very short time to feed them; and that was the reason they thought, 'What's the use of working for a lower price when we could acquire the top value? And even if the price goes down, we won't starve at all because we've got a lot at home that we can live on.'

It just more or less demoralised the whole pearling industry. It wasn't worthwhile working, and the majority of us hopped out to work for the white companies. You were free to go and work for the other companies, but if you worked on the Company Boat, you could not sell your catch to the white companies.

The owners [of the Company Boats] didn't have any option at all. They had to abide by whatever the DNA had to offer. And the other thing that the DNA did was, they'd offer maintenance. Maybe it was good in a way. They offered this low price and then they maintained the boats as well, and whatever catch that came in, half of it went to cover the slipway bills and the repair bills, and the other half paid for the men and the upkeep and the tucker and whatever — running costs.

If this was the government policy, it failed dramatically to cope with the challenge of plastics which destroyed the pearlshell and trochus industries after 1959.

Koiki spoke some more about the charge that was levelled at him. The girl was someone he knew from school and liked.

Actually, I was going to marry this girl, but because of that penalty they imposed on me, I wandered off — you know, came to the mainland.

I asked Koiki how the girl's parents reacted.

Well, it's like the traditional thing. There was hatred, you know;

they hated me for that, and then from that time they kept a very strict eye on her. They wouldn't let her come anywhere near where I was. And that sort of made it difficult for me so I just wandered off and went to Darnley and then found a boat from there; worked on Darnley for a little while, and then occasionally we'd call on Murray. I wasn't able to see that girl again. And then after about twelve months on the *Placid* (that was skippered by Noel Baker) we came back and, for two years after that, I didn't even talk to the girl because of that rule that was imposed on us.

Koiki had the usual range of semi-skilled work on the luggers. This experience began on the Placid.

I was a deckhand on it, and a diver — a skindiver. And we worked for a share. And we had a kind of competition; each one would work for themselves and see how much shell you could collect. I wasn't very good at it because, you know, one of my eyes is shortsighted from when I was a kid and it's important for skindiving. And, you know, I didn't do well in that. I think the biggest lot of shells I've ever picked up in one day was two sackbags. That's eight hours' work. And the weight equivalence would be about two hundredweights. I don't know how much it is in kilos [about 100 kilograms].

I was pretty good at deep-water diving. I went down anything up to 50 feet with just goggles. Fifty feet was the deepest I went down — with no air. You have to hold your breath. I didn't do that to collect shells, but mainly to untie the anchors of the luggers that got tangled up on the coral underneath. I'd take off down and there'd be two or three blokes behind me to watch, to keep an eye on me and to see that no sea snakes or whatever would come near me. And [I'd] untangle the chain and then shoot back up.

Diving suits were not used on the Placid *but they were on other luggers Koiki worked on, although he did not think the Torres Strait Islanders used them.*

After I'd completed the 12 months, [I] came back to Murray. Right, it was actually two years that I stayed there, but instead of staying on Murray I went to TI occasionally and worked for a month or six weeks like that, on another boat, and then I went back home. I did it for two years, off and on.

I didn't do suit diving. I went as a trainee for a month one time in the harbour, to use suit diving, but I didn't go out actually on the pearling boat. I didn't do that. It was only a training, just in the harbour itself, just to get me to get used to the suit. Then I was later instructed by one of the Nona brothers. I just can't remember whether it was Ben Nona or someone else. I knew he was a Nona. And he said to me, 'The suits are difficult to use.'

The Japanese used the suits. They taught the Islanders to use them too, but the Islanders found the suits were much more difficult because of the current. When the current swept anyone against the face of the cliff of coral, and their lifeline got entangled on the coral, there was no way you could signal the tender on the deck; so therefore, you've got to do it fairly quickly — throw the helmet off and try and reach up to the surface. Most of them died by doing that. It's very risky. The Japanese also lost a lot of men, too, over the same thing, because the coral bottom is all up and down like cliffs.

Koiki discussed the depths a diver could descend to in a diving suit. He thought it was 40 fathoms, approximately 73 metres. He, himself, had never done such a dive.

It's a long way down. Only swimming diving was done, skin-diving in other words, for trochus and bêche-de-mer. Swimming diving was done [for pearlshell] on Warrior Reef, and back in what they call the Old Grounds. The Old Grounds are towards Arafura Sea from Boigu in the north, and come down towards Mabuiag and I think there's a cay just south from there. [There was swimming diving in] those areas, and when they had eliminated the catches in those areas, they started working towards the deeper waters of the Eastern Islands; so there were suits used in those waters.

The Master Boats were allowed to pull in to Murray to recruit a crew.

Everybody was allowed [to visit Murray to recruit crew] but, of course, as a matter of courtesy, the skipper would approach the councillors first, and get their okay before they [the councillors] released the crew [to work on the boats]; of course, he [the skipper] took the responsibility. The councillor instructed him. Marou was quite good at that, but none of the blokes would get into strife. There was no drinking. Not on Murray. They could drink *tuba*, but there was no such thing as liquor from TI to be brought by the pearling boats to Murray. They could drink the locally made *tuba*. They could drink that but, you know, no European liquors from TI.

5

Searching for the new life

'Canecutting was a way out to the big country down south'

After being exiled for twelve months Koiki actually did not return to Murray Island to work for two years. He then worked on luggers in the Torres Strait for another two years.

For a few months I stayed on Murray looking for whatever jobs I could pick up locally. Then my mother suggested that there was a boat leaving TI on a certain date that would take men to the cane fields, to cut cane for six months.

It was during Christmas time that I left and came to TI, and instead of joining the boat that was taking the canecutters to Cairns, I decided to join Asera Saveka, because my mates were also signing up on the lugger. Asera was an ex-Murray Islander who lived on St Paul's and I joined him on a boat called *Britain*; and we worked from there to Cairns. We acquired something like 13 tons in six weeks, 13 tons of trochus; and we unloaded in

Cairns. Then I got transferred. The South Sea Pearling Company that owned *Britain* acquired another boat and they wanted half of the crew members to go onto the other one. So I decided to go on the *Triton*. It was skippered by Conny Saveka. Conny was Asera's older son.

So I hopped in with Conny and worked with him. I think I told you the story that we came in to Townsville and I think we had 6 tons on board. Then we wanted to get another ton before we went to Cairns and we worked on Britima and Trunk Reef and all the other reefs around here. We were out on the Trunk on the 29th of June, my birthday; I think I might have been about twenty. Yes, that's right, it was my twentieth birthday and we anchored off this cay. I can't remember the name of the cay now; it was just north-east of Britima Reef, just out here, and I decided — I was kind of a senior to the other fellows — I decided to take the young fellows ashore and just play around on the beach and chase birds and stuff. And while we were there, this big storm came up. We didn't take any notice. We had the pressure light going; we were dancing around and acting the goat. Then we suddenly realised we were hit by a storm and it blew our lamp out, and we came back to where the boat was pulled up on the beach, and tipped the boat up and we hid underneath. And the storm went on for a couple of hours and then, when it slowed down a bit, we thought we would find our way to the boat, to the lugger. And then just as we were rowing across, another storm blew up, and of course the lights on the lugger went off, and we didn't know where we were going. So we started drifting that night. We drifted and drifted until we came on to a reef and I tied the rollock on to a fender of the dinghy and threw it over. It got caught on the coral and held the boat for a while until the tide came up and then of course the waves started to break and we were scared of swamping the boat so I pulled the anchor up and we drifted again. We were drifting west and by dawn we were about five miles off Palm Island. I pulled the canvas out (we had an old canvas on board) and rigged a sail and tied it on to two oars; and the three young fellows with me sat in front, and I sat at the back and steered towards Palm Island. By that time the *Triton* had pulled its anchor up and started looking for us. They went right down towards Dunk Island and then turned around and they picked up a radio message, from another boat called *Antonia*, that they saw us sailing towards the Palms. So they turned around and came back from there and caught us. By about 11 o'clock, they picked us up. We were about five miles or so off Palm Island. They picked us up and took us out again.

The *Triton* was owned by the South Sea Pearling Company, which was a big pearling company. It's a beautiful boat, a beautiful sea boat, and we went working towards Cairns; and then just out of Dunk Island, we ran short of water. So we ran into Lucinda to collect water. That is where I met Kevin Saylor and Tonga Geesu and Remon. And I got a lift on the truck and went to where my [future] wife lived — [she was working at Lucinda as a kitchen hand then] — and met them. And then after that, we went back to Cairns. We worked all the way up there and acquired the extra two tons of shells and went into Cairns to unload.

We unloaded our catch in Cairns; then they were getting ready to leave and I packed up and came the other way. Not only myself, there were five of us I think. We decided to come to Innisfail to get a job cutting cane because we knew some of the Mazas were in Innisfail, someone we knew. Anyway, we had difficulty locating them. Instead we went to a boarding house, and then we went on a pub crawl to see who we could meet. And that is when we ran into the police officers. They were plain dressed policemen. They were informed by the company from

Cairns that we had deserted the boat and come to Innisfail, and they rounded us up and asked us who we were. Instead of staying with the rest of my mates, I sort of went out on my own just a little bit further away from them. The intention was that I would tell them my false name. And I did. I gave my [future] wife's surname to them, Nehow, and told them that I was from Ingham. About an hour later, they came back and we had moved from there to another pub. It might have been about half an hour or so. They came back and picked up all my mates and left me alone. They picked them up and put them on the back of the ute — the police used to have utilities then — and transported them back to Cairns, because of that restriction on the movements of Islanders. I was misleading them by telling them my false name.

I asked Koiki what made him change his mind. Why had he gone back on the luggers instead of cutting sugarcane as he had intended?

My mother wanted me to come down to cut cane, but instead I think there was that peer pressure again. My age group were not going to cut cane, they were going to work on this lugger, so I just joined up with them. But I wrote a letter to my mother, wrote to her and said that instead of going canecutting, I mean to sign on this lugger. She knew the fellow that was in charge of the boat, Asera Saveka. She knew him because they were brought up on Murray, in the same village more or less. After Innisfail I found my way down to Townsville and, at that time, I think I only had about 12 quid in my pocket.

He laughed at the memory of his own youthful daring.

Not from my wages. I assigned my wages to my mother, the time that I spent on the boat. Actually I wrote Killoran a letter and asked him to transfer that money to my mother's account; and he sent me a form back and I signed it and sent it back to them. It was an authority form that transferred the money and cancelled my account with the DNA passbook. During the time when I came to Innisfail the money that I had was actually from the sale of materials that I collected, and a couple of little pearls that I had. I just sold them for £3 each to a taxi driver when I was on TI working with the pearling luggers. The rest of the money was from a sale of cowries and stuff like that for tourists. The taxi driver offered to give me £6 or something, and I gave him the whole box just to get rid of it.

The money that was transferred to my mother's account, that happened twelve months afterwards. So it didn't happen at the same time. It happened twelve months after I acquired a permanent job. After I acquired a job in Townsville, then I wrote to Killoran and asked him to transfer my wage and all the money that I had. I think it was only £97. It was held on Thursday Island. He didn't try to arrest me. That surprised me of course.

I asked Koiki if he was concerned that he might be sent back to the Islands after Killoran learnt of his whereabouts from his letter.

No, I wasn't frightened at all. No, I wasn't concerned about that at all. I knew that his concern was that we must be able to demonstrate that we were capable of looking after ourselves away from the DNA. I think that was the underlying factor and obviously, in my case, I was more than able to look after myself.

I was surprised that Koiki had such a positive view of Killoran and the Queensland Government administration, especially as Koiki had illegally left the boat.

The address that I gave him was my work address, and on the letter I said, 'This is where I am working and will you please forward my money to my mother?' And gave him my mother's name. Then he sent the form back to the same address I had on the top of the letter; and there were no inquiries after that.

I knew that I had some money because I had the book with me from the previous work that I had done and my money went to that account; and I still had it with me. When I had found myself a job, I then opened up a Commonwealth Bank account and then decided that the money that I had on the DNA passbook was no use to me at all. It would be better if my mother used it; and she held a similar passbook on Murray.

I asked Koiki if he had ever been sent back to the Torres Strait by Killoran.

No, he sent my mates back. He never ever sent me back. I went back after Netta and I got married in 1959. In 1960 I went back. Eddie was 18 months old I think. In '61–'62 I went back and had a great conversation with him. He was keen on asking how I got on in the mainland: 'And you managed to get married; and you've got a nice little boy; and you are neatly dressed', and all that kind of stuff. It was only obvious that I liked dressing up. That is how I am.

Q: *Shouldn't you have got his permission to get married?*

I didn't want his permission.

Koiki laughed scornfully at the idea. I asked him if he would have had to get permission when he was on the Islands to get married. At that time Aborigines had to.

No, actually that rule never applied to us.

I married Netta in '59, in August, September; 10 September. No. Not September. October — 10th October we got married. Then eighteen months later my mother was in hospital in TI. I went back to see her and took Eddie with me, and she was able to see Eddie twice. She had tuberculosis, you see. And I sneaked Eddie in just to see the old lady. I sneaked him in a couple of times and then, when I got caught, they told me to keep Eddie, away from his grandmother, just for his benefit. And I did that, kept him away. Then one day I had a long conversation with Paddy Killoran on TI.

It seems that in the Islands and even when they left the Islands and worked on boats and elsewhere, the Islanders had more freedom than the Aborigines would have had from Palm Island or Cherbourg or any of the other government reserves or missions.

Yes, I think that we had much more freedom; for instance there was no restrictions in marriage. You could marry anyone you wanted, except that you couldn't marry a European. A European could not marry an Islander girl. There were no dormitories for orphans or kids without parents. Their traditional way, as soon as the parents went, there was always someone there to take the kids soon after death.

I mentioned the dormitory system that was inflicted on Aboriginal people which Koiki had fleetingly glimpsed when he visited Palm Island. Children who were put in dormitories often had parents, but the Department decided that they weren't suitable parents. Most of the missions had a policy of separating all the children into dormitories to separate them from Aboriginal cultural forces and Aboriginal discipline.

We didn't have that at all. Maybe there was a lack of money to provide the accommodation for that sort of thing, but I do remember there were a couple of occasions when both parents died. Paddy Killoran himself ordered the relatives to take the kids or to send them to the mother and father of the deceased. Paddy Killoran himself, because he understood the relationship and how we care for our young.

I asked Mabo if Killoran was popular with the Islanders, as I understood they called him the King or the Prince of the Torres Strait.

The Prince of the Torres Strait. He was in a way. In a way he was popular because he knows the Islands back to front; and he got on quite well because of his understanding of the culture. But his policies were what I call a shithouse.

Mabo again stressed the difference between these policies and the warm, father-figure administrator.

Oh, yes. For instance, when I first got convicted for drinking on Murray, that meeting we had nearly ended up in a fist fight between him and me. Yes, and I was only very young then. It was a severe argument. Oh, yes. I got so tempered up I could have punched him, but I didn't.

Koiki laughed at his own temerity, especially when I stated the obvious: Killoran was a big man.

He *was* a big man! Well, last time I saw him, I just sort of said good day. It is a long time since we sat around and talked. I was on the National Aboriginal Education Committee and it was a kind of a passing hello and goodbye at Bamaga.

Personally, it is a different matter. I have met him several times and when I was just out of school and was waiting to go on a lugger, I met him several times. By Jesus, he was like a father to me. And even the time when I went to TI, the first thing he asked me was, 'How is your mother? I believe she is in the hospital.'

This was Killoran's method of soft control.

I asked Mabo why his mother had wanted him to take on cane cutting, which was one of the most arduous jobs imaginable.

Well, I think she wanted me to get away from the luggers. Actually it wasn't her wish for me to go on the luggers. She wanted me to do something different from pearling and diving. 'Your dad had done it all his life. It's about time, when you grow up, you do something different, something different from whatever your dad has done. It is a dead end job. You can't gain any other experience except looking at corals and whatever.' Little did she know there was a scientific study going on about the Barrier Reef.

Canecutting was a way out to the big country down south. My dad also went down canecutting. He went down for a short time — six months — and then back again.

Remember I mentioned old Marou, when he worked in Cairns on a delivery cart for Burns Philp. He got to know some of the cane farmers and then when he went back home, when Marou went back home, he had that in his mind. So after the war he got in touch with some of these people. I don't know how he got in touch with them, but he did. Whether he did it through Killoran I don't know, I am not quite sure about that. Then the response was that the cane farmers sent him a radio message to select so many men for the cane season. And he then held a public meeting and said, 'Look, this message I got.' I remember as a kid, when the first lot came down, we sat under an almond tree. It was a big mob of people. I think at that time Murray had about 1500 people still living there, and he stood up and held the paper and gave it to Dougie Geesu I think. He was a police officer and he read the message, and the message said that he wanted to recruit, and asked Marou to recruit eighteen men, I think, to cut cane in Cairns and Gordonvale for six months. So they put a blackboard up and each one that wanted to go and work there, they got up and put their names down. That was soon after the war.

Koiki thought that the first Islanders recruited received a lower wage than other canecutters, because Killoran wanted his cut as well for the Department. I suggested that Killoran probably arranged for the canecutters to go to Cairns.

Yes, I think that might have happened. I think it was an arrangement between the Department office on TI and the cane farmers down in Cairns, and of course the ship. A boat picked them up and brought them to Cairns, and after they finished, I remember a very fast boat by the name of *PK* — it was a kind of patrol boat — delivered the men back to the island. It left Cairns and went straight across to Cape Flattery. And then there is an entrance, a passage between the Barrier Reef on to the Coral Sea, and it headed straight in to Yule Entrance just south of Murray. And that's where it went in and anchored off Murray and all the men came ashore. I remember that because I used to look forward to when my dad came back from the south. He always brought a nice present for us. He would be away for about six months.

When I was sixteen then, my dad had done his back, and he wasn't good enough to come down to Cairns to cut cane again, so he stayed back home and just worked as a cook on the luggers. That's when Mum started talking to me about cutting cane.

I think she thought I might leave the islands for good but she didn't express it, because when I left she was crying her head off.

I got that idea [of leaving the islands for good] at the time when I confronted Killoran — when he told me that I might have to work on the back of his truck for no wages at all for twelve months. That's where I got the idea that you are not going to see me around here any more. I didn't want to work for no wages at all. The restriction of somebody standing over me and telling me that I am not to do this and I am not to do that. That is the thing that made me angry.

I asked Koiki if he had ever officially got 'out from under the Act'? Had he ever applied for permission to be freed from the control of the Act?

No, I never ever applied.

Q: *Did any other Torres Strait Islanders apply?*

Oh, yes. There was quite a few, quite a few I know. My cousin Mapa Kudub officially applied. Because he showed me the exemption that he obtained for it and I have seen it. I don't know where it is now. Maybe his widow still has it. He is dead now, this guy. When I came down here, I didn't worry about applying, I just went to the Electoral Office and registered. There were no questions asked at all.

The other thing too I could add to this, you know how they used to conscript young men and send them across to Korea and Malaya and all that. I got a letter from them. It was after Netta and I were married. No, we didn't get married yet; it was before that. I got a letter from the Defence Department telling me to go and enlist. I went to their Sturt Street office and they said, 'You got the letter?' I showed them the letter and then I told them that I refused to enlist. And they said, 'You know you get into trouble over that.' And I went and saw a fellow by the name of — who was the politician at that time? — [Ernie] Harding I think. I went and saw him and he said, 'Oh, leave it with me, we'll sort it out.' Apparently there was a clause in the Defence Act that no indigenous people were to be conscripted. It was a voluntary thing for them.

Well, I never heard anything from them afterwards. But my

friend Carl Wacando, he just went and enlisted. He got called up but he didn't protest, and he just went in and that was it. And he served two or three years I think. I didn't want to join the Army. I think we were involved in Korea. I just didn't want to be in the Army. But instead I went out west and got myself a job on the construction gang building bridges with Thiess Brothers. They started the rail construction from here to Mount Isa and I joined the Thiess Brothers.

I asked Koiki to elaborate on his early attempts to find work in Townsville. The vision of a young Murray Islander trudging along the railway line north towards Ingham asking each ganger if he had a vacancy fascinated me.

When I first came to Townsville, there was a boarding house that I went and stayed in for a couple of weeks. See, when I came I had twelve quid. I went there and it was ten bob a night at the boarding house and I must have stayed there for about four nights I think. And then my money was running short and I decided I'd better go and look for a job. I was looking for work on the railway line. I went to the office in town and they said the gangers on the fettling gangs would have more idea how many men they would need. 'We would recruit them, but so far we haven't got any information. So if you approached them yourself, ask them to let us know — the Personnel Section — that they are in need of men.' So I packed my swag and threw it on my shoulder and walked towards Rollingstone.

Koiki set out to walk 53 kilometres along the railway line from Townsville to Rollingstone looking for a job. He set out at 5.30 am. If he hadn't found a position by the time he reached Rolling-stone he intended to catch the railmotor back.

I walked along the railway line and then I came to the Garbutt gang and saw the ganger there. There was nothing. And I walked from there to (can't remember the name of the place now) Moselle, no, not Moselle.

I slipped in that this was the name of the wine we had with our meals in Canberra.

Yes, there is a place out west too. I went to this next stop towards Rollingstone and there was another small gang and there was no work. The third gang I came on to, at Saltwater Creek, luckily there was my countryman, David Sam. David Sam was my clansman. We are from the same clan group. It is a sub-clan of the Piadram tribe. And he was apparently there some five years before I arrived, and he was glad to see me. He was the only Islander there. He spoke English a bit. He still can't talk much now. Even today [*laughing indulgently*]. Anyway he took me in. He took me in and said to me, 'Look, I give you a job — you cook for me while you are here.' He was single you see, and still is single. He is about 68 now, I think, or 70. Anyhow, I was glad that he took me in and I cooked for him for about a week. Then, when his pay day came, he said to me, 'I will give you five quid and you go and look for a job in Townsville.' And he did. He put me on a rail motor and sent me back to Townsville.

[In Townsville] I walked into another group of Islanders on the wharf, from a boat by the name of *Robin*. It was a motor vessel. It wasn't a lugger, it was just a launch. It was tied up with a whole lot of Islanders on board and was skippered by Dougie Pitt (Jnr). And the Employment Service was across the road from the wharves, at the end of Flinders Street, and I walked in there.

And this old guy remembered me from before and he interviewed me and he said there was a job at the Harbour Board and would I like to take it? I said, 'Yes, I'll take it.' So I went down there for an interview and they said, 'The job will be ready in a week.' They were pulling the Townsville dredge on to a slip and I thought, 'I am not going to go back to David Sam', so I signed on this lugger for a week, the lugger that I told you was full of Islanders.

It was a boat from Mackay, you see, and it was also taking care of the last bit of price that was left. I think it was only about £120 per ton then for trochus. It was the very bottom of it all. And then, instead of staying for a week, I stayed for three months and missed out on that job down the Harbour Board.

They were all a mixture of Torres Strait Islanders. I think there were two blokes from Saibai, four from Darnley, two from St Paul's. There was quite a mixture of people. Three months. That was bad luck but I enjoyed their company. They were a mob of drunks too. I used to hate it. I used to hate them drinking around the boat. One time we came back into Townsville and unloaded two tons of shells. We got a little bit of money and then we brought our food back and we put the rations and stuff into the boat and took off again. It was six o'clock in the afternoon when we left the harbour. And all the fellas were drunk, and at that time I was the youngest then, the youngest of the whole lot — I must have been about 21 or 22 then — and we left the harbour and started sailing towards Hayman Island and on the way towards Cape Cleveland, they all went to sleep and left me and another guy and the white engineer by the name of Barry. (I can't remember his second name now. I see him sometimes sell pies on the side of the road here. He lost his leg during the war. He was on crutches.) Anyway, there were only three of us and he was down below in the engine room and me and this other young fellow were steering the boat away merrily as we went. Then we went out to Cape Cleveland and the weather blew up. It was about twelve o'clock. I was sort of steering and falling off to sleep and then I'd wake up and turn it back to the right course again. Anyway this time I woke up and found the boat heading towards the mainland. I realised we were in very small water and that small water was caused by Cape Upstart that runs across, and we were right in the middle of that heading towards it. And then, when I looked towards the horizon, I could see dark patches, trees, and I started turning the boat away from it. And while I started turning the boat away, it just ran aground bang on its side. Luckily it was just sand bar underneath and of course everybody left their bunks and came up on to the deck then.

6

Being black in North Queensland

'You'd do your own battling'

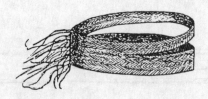

When I was a kid growing up, one of the things that my uncle taught me was to make dugouts out of wood. I was really young then.

We rigged the dugout canoe up fully the way they used to have it, the traditional sailing canoe. And we used to go out fishing, mainly around the home reef on Murray. Then after a while he'd pull the sails down and we just used to paddle, paddle out with outriggers on it. That was during the war years. My mother used to use it a lot. She used to go out after what they call rock cods. At a certain time of the year the rock cod comes out on Murray in abundance. Got some reef fish to eat too. We ceased to use the dugout canoe, but that was the only training I had. Actually I picked navigation up from my dad when occasionally he would work on the dinghies, sailing dinghies. And I'd go out with him for a day or two, and I got used to sailing, sailing with just a sail boat, no motor on it. And then, when I came to TI, then all they did was to teach us to read compasses with north, south, east and west and how to read charts, how to get from one reef to the other. That was the only thing they taught us and for radio things, mainly to turn it on and turn to the frequency, or whatever, and just listen to it and how to press the thing before you talk. That was the only thing they taught us.

I asked Koiki what had happened after his boat was beached at Cape Upstart.

We got it afloat. See, when the tide came in we put all the dugong spears they had on board, put them on the sides. As the tide came up we kept lifting the boat up on the side it was on. We kept pushing it up, [using the dugong spears] as props until it was afloat. Then we started the motor and reversed it out.

It was owned by a fellow by the name of Kirkpatrick. They were getting the last of the trochus market. I stayed three months and earned about £50, £50 and keep. Then after that, of course, I came back to Townsville and asked for a job there. Back to the Harbour Board, and they offered me the same thing, same job. Actually I came back three times and got the same job.

I went there first time and I got it. Then I went away to cut cane in Innisfail and came back. Walked into the same job. Then, by that time, it was a tug hand, deck hand on a tug. And then left and went out west and came back. That was the third time. I walked into the same job. Tommy Lafferty was a personnel officer and he got very fond of me, you know.

And then I left them again and married Netta and went out west, then came back. You know, when you're young — I didn't have any desire to hold a permanent job. You know, whenever the pressure grew, my peer group went. I went with them as well. Maybe I just wanted to wander around and see the rest of the place [the mainland] before I could settle down in a permanent job.

Oh, life on the luggers was good, I enjoyed it, but the [working] conditions I did not. You'd start six o'clock in the morning. You're wet from six until six at night, or possibly ten, eleven o'clock at night. Very long hours. But the life itself was good. And I was able to get on with the rest of the crew members, and we had a wonderful time, especially when we went in to places like Palm Island. The restrictions on Palm Island really surprised me. We had nothing like that on Murray.

We discussed the different way the Queensland Government administration treated the Torres Strait Islanders and the Aborigines. To me, Islanders were treated with more consideration than were the Aborigines, but this preferential treatment became a means of soft control. After the Torres Strait Islander maritime strike of 1936, Torres Strait Islander councils were given some local government authority. However, under the Directors of Aboriginal and Islander Affairs, O'Leary and Killoran, this personalised involvement with the Islanders became so effective a form of soft control that, in the 1960s the leading activists in the protest movement were nearly all Aboriginal. Geography and language added to the Islanders' political isolation, cutting them off to a large extent from the supportive black, white and multiracial organisations and pressure groups in the southern capital cities. Mabo qualified this assessment, once again emphasising the importance of the mastery of the English language.

I think what happened there is that English is our second language, whereas, for the generation of Aborigines that took that political role, English was their first language, and they found it less difficult. They had less difficulty in communicating or getting the message across to the Europeans, whereas we're still going through the same problem. People like myself (who have [an Islander] language) have, you know, used English so long that we can assert ourselves in a political way.

The differential treatment of Torres Strait Islanders was some-times reflected in their relations with officials on the mainland. In Innisfail in 1957 the police allowed Islanders to drink in the pubs even though all, including Koiki, were still 'under the Act'. It would have been illegal for them to drink alcohol and illegal for the publican to sell it to them. At the time of the 1939 Torres Strait Islanders Act, the possibility of Islanders seeking exemp-tion was not allowed for, as they were all confined to the Torres Strait, nearly all living on their own islands.

Well, in Innisfail we were allowed to go into pubs drinking because there were Islanders already in Innisfail, like Mazas. Mazas went over from Palms. They were sent across. Not the Maza I told you about that owned the lugger, *Adai*, up there, but his brother, his older brother.

And his brother was sent across to open up Palm Island even many years before the war, and he then was exempted, I think, from Palm and he went and lived in Innisfail.

And when we came, there was no such thing as barring people, barring Blacks from the pub in Innisfail. Actually I didn't meet any Aborigines at this time.

No one ever knocked us back. No. And then, I don't know, perhaps they never seen a Torres Strait Islander before. I'm not sure. But Mazas were there before us. Bob was only a schoolboy, Bob Maza, now with the theatre company in Sydney, he was only a schoolboy at that time. They're Murray Islanders too. They were born on Palms, and bred up in the urban scene around Innisfail and Cairns.

After the Innisfail episode, I came to Townsville and worked on the lugger *Grobin*; then joined the Harbour Board again, then left them. Went to the canefields and it was in '58 when I actually met Bonita. She was still at school [when Koiki first visited the South Sea Islander village at Halifax, the Gardens]. And then in '58 and '59 I came back to the Harbour Board and we went out west.

Netta informed me that Koiki was wrong about her being at school. She was working when she first met Koiki.

I didn't like the west much because there was nothing there. My only intention was that it was a job that I hang on to and save enough money to come back in here [to Townsville].

It was something totally different. Actually, when I got up, I thought I was back on the luggers, because when you get up in a lugger and you look across, all you see is water and nothing else around it. That's what I thought when I was on the plains and looked around. There were no trees except on the hills way up in the distance. It was like an island, just coming out of the horizon. That's the impression I got. Then, after a while, I got used to it.

I didn't like it. Mainly the isolation and the heat, I think, and the cold in the winter. *That* I didn't like. I started off [working] in a place called Prairie when I joined the Thiess Brothers, Thiess Brothers and Hornibrooks. A lot of my countrymen were on Hornibrooks and I joined the Thiess Brothers. And then I went from there to Hughenden; then on to Marathon. And I left them, left Thiess Brothers, and came back to Hughenden, and got on to a fettling gang for a few months with another Islander called Wya George. We used to spell it Wya but it was a short name for Waida.

And I joined him a few months, then I left. Bonita got pregnant with Eddie and she was nine months when I sent her in to

Three Meriam elders, late 1890s. (from A.C. Haddon, *Reports of the Cambridge Anthropological Expedition to the Torres Strait*, Cambridge University Press, 1908–1935)

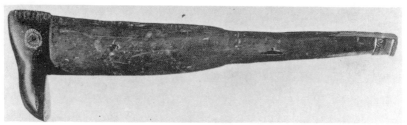

Meriam club (above). Meriam in dance costumes, 1890s (below). (from Haddon)

The traditional Meriam pipe, *zoob*, late 1890s. (from Haddon)

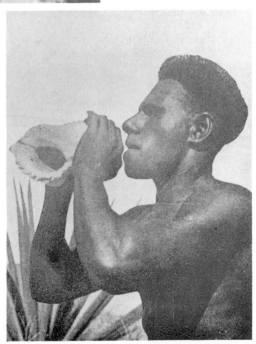

Blowing the *boo* shell, late 1890s. (from Haddon)

The traditional Meriam house. (from Haddon)

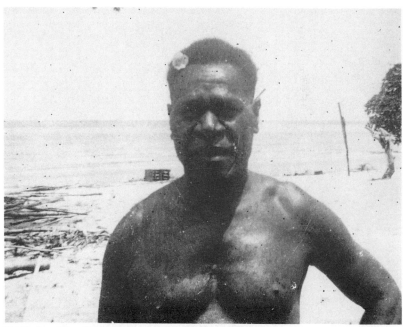

Pai Kaniu at Kiam Village, Mer, 1940s. (Bonita Mabo Collection)

Dela Mopwali, Meriam elder. (Bonita Mabo Collection)

Meriam elder Ogam (Dow Tom), brother of Dela Mopwali, outside his Murray Island home. (Bonita Mabo Collection)

Koiki's sister, Marinda (centre back), Wanee Mabo (front) and Betty Mabo (second front row, right) with the Akee children at Thursday Island, 1961, when Koiki and Bonita were visiting Maiga Mabo in hospital to show young Eddie to his grandparents. Wanee and Betty were adopted by Koiki and Bonita. (Bonita Mabo Collection)

Robert Victor (Bob) Miles, Koiki's admired schoolteacher, in 1945 before he went to Murray Island. He taught Koiki about 'mainland' culture and the importance of English, and learned Miriam from Koiki.
(Courtesy Joan Miles)

Bob Miles at one of his Torres Strait Island schools (probably Yorke Island), around 1950. Koiki Mabo was assistant teacher at Yorke.
(Courtesy Joan Miles)

Sixteen-year-old Koiki at Mer, nursing Susan Cook. (Bonita Mabo Collection)

A Meriam gathering at Murray Island, 1944. (Bonita Mabo Collection)

Maiga Mabo, Koiki's adoptive mother, and Bonita Mabo (back row) with Mrs
A. Gesah and daughter (front) on the hospital steps at Thursday Island.
(Photograph by Koiki Mabo. Bonita Mabo Collection)

Benny and Maiga Mabo (front) with Ezra and Jessie Tapau and baby daughter Wanee, Mer, 1950s. Jessie, Koiki's biological sister, also adopted by Benny and Maiga, died soon after this photograph was taken and Wanee was adopted by Koiki and Bonita. (Bonita Mabo Collection)

Koiki's cousin, the young George Kudub, at Mer. (Bonita Mabo Collection)

Trochus boat with Meriam crew. Benny Mabo, Koiki's adoptive father, worked on this boat. (Bonita Mabo Collection)

The Meriam crew of a trochus shell boat. Benny Mabo is at the extreme right, leaning on the large drum. (Bonita Mabo Collection)

The Mabo wedding, 10 October 1959. Left to right: Raymond Geesu, Monica Saylor, Koiki and Bonita Mabo, Frank Lancini, Gillian Cassady, Benny Bennyfather, Benny Devow (pageboy), Victoria Tanna (flowergirl). (Bonita Mabo Collection)

'I remember wearing his hat and his big boots down the streets of Murray, pretending to be a soldier, without knowing he was my biological dad.' Robert Sambo, Koiki Mabo's biological father, with his second wife, Dai. (Bonita Mabo Collection)

Gail Mabo and Tom David leap for the ball, at play at the Black Community School, around 1980. (Photograph by Koiki Mabo. Bonita Mabo Collection)

The Black Community School moved to a number of temporary sites in its last years. Here it is at Boundary Street, South Townsville. Celuia Mabo is at front left. (Photograph by Koiki Mabo. Bonita Mabo Collection)

Maleta Mabo (second right) and Margaret Tapim watch as their work is corrected, Black Community School, around 1980. (Bonita Mabo Collection)

The Black Community School at 41 Nelson Street, South Townsville in 1980. Koiki Mabo is in the shorts in the centre of the picture. (Bonita Mabo Collection)

Koiki Mabo with children at the Black Community School, 1980. (Bonita Mabo Collection)

Repairing the wall of one of the fish traps on Mer. Children from the Black Community School were on an educational visit back home. (Photograph by Koiki Mabo. Bonita Mabo Collection)

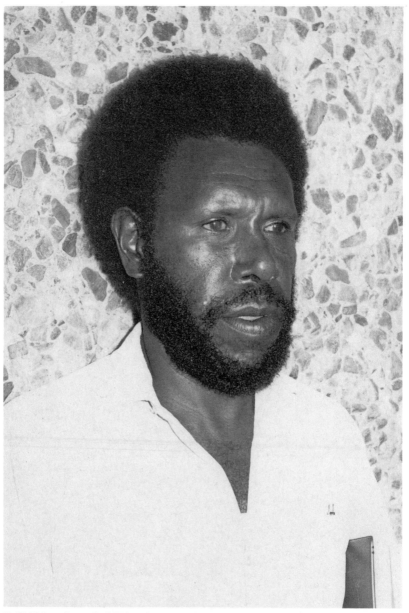

Koiki Mabo at James Cook University, as guest lecturer in Noel Loos's race relations course. (Mabo Collection, Department of History and Politics, James Cook University)

Koiki Mabo teaching students about Torres Strait Islander culture at James Cook University, around 1975. He is holding a *weris*, a fish scoop. Items of Aboriginal culture are in the background. (Mabo Collection, Department of History and Politics, James Cook University)

Koiki Mabo with the then Mayor of Townsville, Mike Reynolds (second left), Josephine Sailor, prominent Aboriginal activist (centre front), and other members of the fifth Festival of Pacific Arts Board of Directors, Townsville, 1988. (Bonita Mabo Collection)

Koiki Mabo with Jack Wailu, a relative and close friend, whose family reside at Las. (Courtesy Yarra Bank Films/Photographer Trevor Graham)

Mabo with his lawyers (Greg McIntyre, left, and Bryan Keon-Cohen, right) at Murray Island during the Queensland Supreme Court hearing. (Courtesy Yarra Bank Films/Photographer Trevor Graham)

Koiki Mabo, a year before his death. (Photograph by Bethel Mabo Duncan, Bonita Mabo Collection)

Koiki Mabo with Murray Island witnesses during the 1989 Supreme Court hearings on Mer. (Courtesy Yarra Bank Films/Photographer Trevor Graham)

Bonita Mabo with daughters Bethel (standing) and Maleta at Koiki's grave in 1992, just after the High Court decision. (Bonita Mabo Collection)

Bonita Mabo receiving the Human Rights Award on behalf of Koiki, with Rev. Dave Passi (left) and Barbara Hocking (right). (Bonita Mabo Collection)

Bonita Mabo with Minister for Aboriginal Affairs, Robert Tickner (left), Lois O'Donoghue, Chairperson ATSIC, and Prime Minister Paul Keating (right), Sydney, 26 January 1993. Koiki had been awarded the 1992 Australian Achiever medallion by the National Australia Day Council. (Photograph by Maleta Mabo. Bonita Mabo Collection)

Meriam Shark Dancers lead the march to the Townsville Mall in honour of Koiki Mabo to celebrate the third anniversary of the High Court decision and Mabo's tombstone unveiling on 3 June 1995. (Courtesy *Townsville Bulletin*)

Aboriginal and Islander supporters of the Meriam march on 3 June 1995. Mick Miller, prominent Aboriginal activist, is at the centre of the Aboriginal flag with Mrs Gladys Tybingoompa of Aurukun (right) beside him. (Courtesy *Townsville Bulletin*)

Bonita Mabo at the tombstone unveiling in Townsville, 3 June 1996. Below the bust of Mabo are the Torres Strait Island pigeon and shark, totems associated with Koiki's Piadram clan. (Courtesy *Townsville Bulletin*)

Eddie Mabo Jr with Koiki's grandson Joel at the march celebrating Mabo's achievements, 3 June 1995. Jim Akee, in sunglasses and hat, leader of the Mer secession movement, is behind Kaleb. (Courtesy *Townsville Bulletin*)

The grieving begins again. Bonita Mabo at the graveside on the morning the desecration of the grave was discovered. (Courtesy *Townsville Bulletin*)

The inexpressible horror of a hatred so deep. Mabo's nephew Sam Wailu, a Murray Island elder (left), with Donald Whaleboat, Koiki's cousin, at the desecrated grave. (Courtesy *Townsville Bulletin*)

The body of Koiki Mabo is carried by Meriam warriors along a narrow path to lie in state for three days at his village, Las, before the burial and tombstone unveiling on Murray Island. (Photograph by Kirsty Alfredson)

Koiki's coffin is about to be lowered into the vault at Las, his final resting place. (Courtesy Film Australia, National Interest Program/ Photographer Trevor Graham)

The grave and veiled tombstone of Koiki Mabo before it was sealed with a marble slab. (Photograph by Kirsty Alfredson)

The great god Malo patrols his domain, to the slow beat of the drums of Mer. The Malo dances, which had not been performed for eighty years, celebrated the spiritual leadership of Koiki Mabo at his tombstone unveiling on Mer. (Photograph by Kirsty Alfredson)

Malo dance at the tombstone unveiling celebrations, Townsville, 3 June 1995. (Photograph by Noel Loos)

The Mabo family, 6 August 1995. Back row: Bethel Duncan, Gail Mabo, Celuia Mabo, Maleta West, Mal Mabo, Wanee Laczik, Eddie Mabo Jr. Front row: Bonita (Netta) Mabo, Maria (Jessie) Mabo. Absent are Mario and Ezra Mabo. (Photograph by Gay Woods, National Library)

On 19 September 1995 the tombstone was unveiled again on Mer. For Bonita Mabo and son Ezra, it was the end of grieving, 'the end of sorry', as Donald Whaleboat explained. (Courtesy Film Australia, National Interest Program/Photographer Trevor Graham)

Ingham. Then I went to the other gang. I joined the bridge gang in the railway itself.

Yes, a fettling gang and then after I joined the Thiess Brothers I came back and got a job down in Jardine Valley with Waida George at Hughenden.

We were stationed at Jardine Valley, a little siding and I was on a flying gang, just working between Prairie and Hughenden and sometimes we went out towards Winton way for about nine months, or not quite nine months (about six months I think). Then Netta came in this way [to Townsville] and I went out; I applied to the bridge gang. That was mainly to get away from Waida George because I couldn't get on with him. We used to fight nearly every day and argue. He was a slavedriver. He was a ganger. Then, when he took over the flying gang, he became a supervisor. All he used to do was just drive around the tracks and look at everybody work. And then I left that gang and went on to a bridge gang for about three months, I think. Then I went to Marathon to another gang out there. Eddie was three years old and Maria was twelve months when we came back to Townsville.

It was mainly repairing. Repairing sleepers and, sort of, getting jobs. It was all right for someone who likes that kind of job. I liked it when I first went out there, mainly because it was different. Then after a while, I got bored.

And the other thing that worried me was that the people I worked with were heavy drinkers. Oh, they drank, I tell you.

I did too for a while. Then I realised that I was making the publicans richer than I was. Then I stopped drinking. Not stopped altogether; I used to buy it and take it home. You know, buy a bottle of wine or something or a carton of grog. We used to get big bottles in those days. And I tell you that would last me for a week, anyway. And then the following week I had no liquor at all, and then on paydays I'd go in and do the same thing. But when we got married, Netta was very religious. She wouldn't allow any grog in the fridge.

So what I did was to have a bottle of claret under the safe in the kitchen, so I used to drink that before tea anyway.

He laughed, remembering how he had to conform to his young wife's wishes.

Netta still has that kind of religious thing. Every time I talk about the Catholics or the Assemblies of God, she sort of looks funny to me. Today, she goes to church whenever she is not tired.

Netta is Assembly of God. When we came to Townsville, she was still very religious then. What I used to do, when I used to live just down from the Catholic Church, I'd drive her to the Assemblies of God Church and leave her there, and then come back, say about 10 o'clock at night on Sundays, and pick her up and take her home.

I'm an Anglican. I used to go too, on Sundays at times. I used to wander off to the Cathedral for mass in Townsville. Sometimes I just felt that I should go to church; just wander off. I went a couple of times to Rising Sun, St Matthew's; a couple of times to St Matthew's. Before this fellow became involved with us in the Inter-Racial Seminar. Clarkson.

The Reverend John Clarkson, then Rector at St Matthew's Anglican Church, Townsville, was one of the clergy active in the 1967 Inter-Racial Seminar, an event first suggested by Koiki. Clarkson had earlier invited the Torres Strait Islander priest, The Rev Boggo Pilot, to preach at St Matthew's.

I remember when Boggo Pilot came through one time from Brisbane. He [Father John Clarkson] took him in there and

[Boggo Pilot] did a sermon or a mass or something. Then he went to Brisbane.

Early work experience

The engineer [on the luggers] was on top wage. He was paid more than even the skipper. And the deck hand wage when I first started off was £15 a month. That went on for a couple of years. Then, the final year that I worked on the *Triton*, it was £17.

There were white blokes employed in the shell stores when we came in to unload. They were the ones that delivered all the bags to us and helped us pack the shells in and then transport it away to the export market.

Koiki worked with other Torres Strait Islanders and had limited contact with white workers in the industry.

But I think that the blokes that worked in the industry, although I didn't ask them how much wage they earned, I would presume they were paid the award rates. I think it might have been about £20, £20 a week wages then.

Immediately Koiki left school his competency in English was recognised. As he mentioned earlier, when he was fourteen or fifteen, he worked for a medical team as an interpreter, mainly asking questions of Islanders in Torres Strait Islander Kriol. He was also appointed as a schoolteacher at Yorke Island, by Robert Miles, teaching, in his words, 'the littlies', the infant class. At this time there was no training for Torres Strait Islander teachers except their own school experience and the supervision of the white teachers they were attached to.

It was the schoolteacher Robert Miles that told me before I left the Islands that the plastics, synthetics, were being introduced. The colour was much the same as shell buttons. So the shell would not last for too long and they knew it was on the down run then. I was glad that I was already on the mainland when the bottom completely fell out [of the market] because I'd already acquired knowledge of other jobs and even unskilled work. I'd already acquired skill to do that.

When Koiki first started working in Townsville, he thought he was the only Torres Strait Islander in the city. There were a number already employed on the western railway line.

There were none in Townsville, but there were quite a few, might have been about fifty or so, just between here and Charters Towers on that rail construction when the Hornibrook started. They had one lot of camps somewhere around Mingela, and there was one lot in Charters Towers. There were other camps further up, and there were Islanders coming into Townsville for the weekend. And I didn't like them because they were mad drinkers too. I didn't like them because they went crazy on grog. All the money they got, they just came into the pub and blew it all.

This was a mixed group from a number of Islands.

But it was my lot that I actually started talking to about taking more care of your money. It was okay back home. You can go home and give all your money to your parents and have nothing for yourself because you know that, up there in the gardens, you've got sweet potatoes and bananas growing. You can go and get it and eat it. But here [on the mainland], you can't. You've got to rely on whatever money you can get. We came from a community where there was no such thing as liquor on hand, and when we did find a place that you could have liquor any time of the day that you want it, they sort of became crazy about it for a while and drank every weekend, although they knew that they had to work. I was proud that they did have a motive to work.

But as soon as they stopped work the first thing they did was race off to the pub; and you could do better without it.

It's gone out now, except very young people now just come out of school. They do that, but not when you get up to, say, the age of twenty or twenty-one; hardly anyone does it. But it was a novelty at the time.

The situation in Townsville with regards to the consumption of alcohol by adult Torres Strait Islanders seems, in the 1990s, to be still surprisingly restrained and controlled, surprising in comparison with the white community. At three social functions I have attended, two celebrating the Mabo Decision and the other a wedding, no Torres Strait Islanders were drinking alcohol at the functions and very few were away from the crowds in an adjacent hotel. At the 1996 Mabo Day feast in the Greek Community Hall only a few elders went to the bar to have an occasional drink. My guess is that the consumption of alcohol is much less among Torres Strait Islanders than among white Australians. The Islanders can certainly have a good time without alcohol as a social lubricant.

They used to get me upset and I'd take off before the weekend came; say, Friday night I used to take off from the boarding house to a friend of mine that I met. He was a fireman on one of the tugs, on the *Lalor*. And I used to take off with him to go out fishing and spend all weekend out on Cattle Creek fishing just to get away from this, from my own mob.

I asked what the first group of Torres Strait Islanders (the ones who had taken the Aboriginal girls from the dormitories) were doing at Palm Island.

Well, actually they were on luggers too. They were on the luggers and they apparently went there and somehow the police officers didn't keep a constant watch on them and, of course, any young men would feel like that after being out on the sea for twelve weeks. And then I guess you'd be attracted. And because of that, they just walked in and there were women for waste. [*They knew that Palm Island was there?*]. Some of them knew; you know, Islanders have been roaming the Queensland east coast since, maybe, the 1920s. They knew what it was. We knew they were Aboriginal people and, of course, the other thing derogatory is that it goes back to the traditional thing: that they weren't [believed to be] culturally advanced. It was our traditional opinion.

Culturally they were thought to be inferior. I think the idea is going out now. Yes, not so much now as it was. Mainly because of mixed marriages now, and just things gone out. But it was very strong in those days, back in the '50s just to label anyone as an Aboriginal. There's a word for it in our Meriam language, a word *agai*, meaning an Aboriginal, which would be an insult. *Agai* [only] means native of Cape York.

It's like calling someone a Black. That sort of term, or a nigger. And we've got another term for Papua New Guineans. It's a native word for people from that area. *Gebarobi*. It means a native of Papua New Guinea.

Koiki felt obliged to explain how the term agai *had become a derogatory one used to imply a person inferior to the Meriam.*

The term *agai* is not a derogatory term. It's our name for people from that land; it's like saying Malaysians or Englishmen, say, British, like that. It depends how you say it. You know, sometimes people say, 'You're as bad as these people.' You know, 'You're as bad as the *Agais*.' Then it becomes derogatory. But the word itself is not derogatory. It's like me calling myself Meriam. I'm a Meriam. The Western Islander would also make it derogatory. If they classify one of their people, and say, for instance, if he sang differently, 'Oh, you're singing like a Meriam', then it becomes a derogatory term.

When I was a kid growing up they [the Aborigines] were regarded as lesser beings mainly because they didn't know the art of cultivation and they didn't live in central villages like we did, and they didn't have a religion. We didn't understand that.

And, with their sophisticated weapons, it was surprising to the Islanders, their boomerang and spear. And we couldn't work out how they did it.

I think you still have the friction. There's no way you're going to bring them together. I don't think it'll ever come. As soon as kids finish schooling and get interested in more of an adult life, the friction comes into existence. I couldn't really overcome it [at the Black Community School] mainly because kids, growing up and going working, [understand] the competition that they have for the same goods in the same pot, like houses and jobs.

Koiki is referring to the housing made available to Aboriginal and Islander people and the jobs in government departments or government-supported voluntary organisations such as the Aboriginal and Islander housing cooperatives and legal aid services. Koiki believed Islanders' needs were swamped by the needs of the larger Aboriginal minority and their greater political clout in the distribution of limited resources. This comment was made in November 1984. He went on to repeat his charge that Islanders of this time were only given token consideration.

We've been a label so far, a quote in somebody's letterhead. It's time that we started taking out the ropes [that bind the two indigenous groups together].

Q: *What did you think about the situation for Aborigines on Palm Island and your being made to sit offshore for so long?*

Well, I thought it was funny. I never experienced anything like it, not back at home, not at Murray or anywhere. Just hanging around in a way. It was amazing, but actually I didn't think anything of it. I just accepted it as a rule of that place.

Partly as a result of his confidence in himself and partly through naïveté, Koiki accepted the Palm Island situation as more akin to a police state than the community situation he had known on Murray Island. He found the treatment of the Torres Strait Islanders by the white administration amusing, accepted that this was the way an Aboriginal settlement was run, and thought his crew were suffering for the social and sexual 'misdemean- ours' of the previous Torres Strait Islander lugger. All Islanders were then stereotyped by the Palm Island administration as potential troublemakers, just as Islanders stereotyped the Abo- riginal people they had very little contact with at this time. Yet the Torres Strait Islanders and the Aboriginal women partici- pated willingly in this liberation from their dormitory. A shout from the women would have brought the authorities to their defence and put the young Islander men to flight. This did not happen. The Islander men were liberators of the Aboriginal women from the control and mores imposed by the white admini- stration, if only for a brief time. It was an exuberant defiance of the colonial regime by Aboriginal and Torres Strait Islander youth, who were not intimidated by any fear of the consequences.

Q: *Are you saying that you just thought it was the rules of that particular island, Palm Island in this case?*

Yes. But to me it was amusing. The same thing happened when we went to places like Dunk Island and Hayman, the tourist islands. There were certain times that we were allowed to go ashore, mainly because there were the dances on or we made a particular request to the manager that we were willing to do any odd jobs around the place; and they gave us a certain time to come. And when we went to Palm Island, that's the thought I had: 'Well, this is the time they told us to come and we'll go at that time.'

Q: *You were supervised everywhere by the Aboriginal police. What did you think of them?*

I thought it was also strange, because we had Black Police up there as well but they didn't sort of supervise anybody that arrived on Murray. And I thought that was severe and it restricted our movements and restricted us from seeing some other people that we knew on the island, people like Asan Sam and the Baira family and the Geesu family. We were restricted from visiting them. I mean they were our countrymen and people from back home but we weren't allowed to see them.

Q: *Do the Islander police on Murray take their job seriously?*

Oh yes, they really took it seriously. Actually, my dad was a police sergeant at one stage, too, and he took it very seriously. There were resentments at times, depending on the treatment that they gave to certain young people. Sometimes, for instance when I got caught that time, one of the young fellows put up a fight, and, of course, the police arrested him and gave him a couple of good whacks under the ribs before they locked him up. And, of course, he resented that all the time really after that. But it was actually his fault.

Q: *Was there any resentment that Islander police were enforcing the white man's law?*

There was. There was, but at the same time, they knew from their traditional times that law and order must be obeyed. So someone had to carry it out. See, prior to that we had the *baizam buai*. They were *keparem le*, people who carried the staff, the long stick. Well, those sticks were actually spears. They were a kind of policeman.

Tamer le were part of the sacred society but they participated in the *Tamer* ceremony, the clansmen who participated in *Tamer*.

They [the *baizam buai*] were the actual *keparem le*. They played that role as the *keparem le*. In other words, although they didn't appear in front of the public, they were the sharks of the rainforest, that attacked people who didn't obey the laws. They would attack you without first appearing to you to tell you that you did the wrong thing.

Baizam means a shark. Our word for *baizam* is shark. They were people who hid behind the bushes. Sharks — *baizam* — was our totem, who carried out the laws of the *Agud*. Those same people, *baizam buai*, were the *keparem le* as well. *Baizam buai* is a group of people who belonged to the shark clan. And by becoming *keparem le,* they participated in the cult, in the *zogo* ceremonies, and also policed the islands and carried out the law to make sure that the law of Malo was obeyed and carried out.

Q: *How did you find out all of this?*

My father and my grandfather. Well, actually, when the performance would come, when they would perform, we'd see different people playing different parts in the ceremonies.

Then, when my grandfather was alive, I would ask him to explain what role these men played. And he would explain these men had a certain role in the society; that they do that. And those *keparem le* also were guards at the initiation ceremonies.

See, what made me think about those *keparem le* was that if the white men had not come for at least, say, another hundred years, we would have had those men on a full-time basis, because they were already being employed as guards, for the six months of the initiation period. Food was supplied to them by the *tebud* of the *zogo le*. *Tebud* means 'a friend'. Friends of the *zogo*, friends of the cult. They were being fed and everything was done for them. And their job was to police the whole area to make sure that nobody intruded while the ceremonies were on. They would have become full-time policemen.

The London Missionary society (LMS) had brought Christianity to the Torres Strait Islands in 1871, using Polynesian evangelists from the Loyalty Islands. The arrival at Darnley Island is commemorated on 1 July each year as the 'Coming of the Light'. These ceremonies were performed by Islanders who were committed Christians, as their ancestors had been for at least the previous sixty years. There were no white missionaries living on Murray Island during Koiki's childhood, or indeed since, and the Bishop was over 200 kilometres away at Thursday Island. The church had had Islander priests for generations. In this way Christianity had ceased being the religion of the missionaries. It was unmistakably the *Torres Strait Islander religion, but aspects of the old faith persisted.*

We had Island priests. We had Joseph Lui. When I was born, he baptised me. Joseph Lui. Actually he was my uncle on my mother's side. And then we had Poi Passi who was a cousin of Joseph Lui's, and also a cousin of my mother's too. Their fathers and their mothers were brothers and sisters. And they were also associated there with the descendants, I mentioned, descendants of Gamalai. His other name was Segar and he went to Dauar, to Giar Pit, to Moa, and settled on Giar Pit. Giar Pit is a place on Dauar Island.[1] They were the descendants and they also became very emotional when the traditional ceremonies were held, even though they were practising Christians and fully ordained priests in the Anglican Church.

Koiki's involvement in the trade union movement

I asked Koiki to elaborate on his involvement with the trade union movement.

I think it was in the early sixties when we first established the Advancement League, the Aboriginal Advancement League. Everybody would look at me as a red commo. The Advancement League was regarded as a Communist organisation, by Liberals and any white people around the place. And even up to now, when I reflect my mind back, there were no white people that volunteered to assist us in the Aboriginal Advancement League, not on the local scene. Maybe it was good in a way. Later on, toward 1966 I think, Labor members became members of the Federal Council; Gordon Bryant, for instance, was a Federal Vice-President. Well, you know, at that time we were regarded as a red rag. And then I thought it was important to have white people as well, so we approached the trade unions. And there was a fellow by the name of Eddie Heilbronn, working down the Harbour Board. After, I talked to him; he wanted to know what the Advancement League was doing and so on. And I talked to him and he suggested that I approach Gill, a fellow by the name of Jim Gill, who was Secretary of the Trades and Labour Council. I later learned he was a member of the Communist Party as well. And he [Eddie Heilbronn] suggested that I approach him to see if we could get representation of the Advancement League in the trade union movement. And when I did, they discussed it in the trade union. We got a letter signed by Bill Irving, I think.

And there was an old fellow by the name of Paterson. Paterson or Peterson. I think he was a meatworker. He lived over Railway Estate. Anyway, it was a letter signed by those two men, suggesting that we send two representatives. And Dick Hoolihan and myself were nominated and we became members of the Trades and Labour Council. And, of course, we sort of met regularly with the trade unions. That's what I meant by becoming involved with them.

That was the biggest breakthrough I made in learning about politics, Australian politics. To me it was very important and they sort of made way for me to attend labour conferences. Right. And there was a labour conference held, I think, a couple of times in Townsville. I even went to the Communist conference. The Queensland Communist Party would have their conference and they would ask us to go, me and Dick Hoolihan. And sometimes there were other members like Tommy Sullivan and another old fellow, another old guy. Tommy Sullivan was an Aboriginal. And Saulo Waia. Saulo Waia was another Islander. You know they would nominate either one of us. Always we sort of attended in pairs. I think that was the starting off point of my political involvement in organisations.

It was at that time when we thought about the Inter-Racial Seminar. We then approached the Trades and Labour Council for assistance to follow up the referendum. Then they said the Labour Council would take it up with the Mayor, Angus Smith. Angus Smith or Harold somebody? Harold Phillips. Lucky Harold Phillips. And we did eventually succeed in convincing them. And of course that led on to the stuff that you and I got involved with, the whole thing.

This was the 1967 Inter-Racial Seminar which Koiki initiated. He thought the time was ripe after the success of the 1967 Referendum. This greatly advanced Aboriginal and Torres Strait

Islander civil rights by allowing them to be officially counted in the Commonwealth Census and by enabling the Commonwealth Government to legislate on their behalf and to develop an administrative structure to implement Commonwealth programs. Previously these measures had been specifically prevented by the Commonwealth Constitution. Consequently, in 1967, for the first time since Federation, the Commonwealth was able to take responsibility for its indigenous citizens.

Mabo suggested to his allies in the trade union movement the need for a conference to involve a wide spectrum of the residents of North Queensland so that they could discover the problems confronting black Australians. Three hundred black and white participants came together for a weekend for the first time as equals, responding to four keynote speakers, two black and two white. Prior to the conference, teams had surveyed areas such as Aboriginal and Islander employment, education and housing in Townsville and their findings were reported to the conference. The organising committee consisted of both black and white residents of Townsville, including Koiki, and representatives from the trade union movement, James Cook University and the churches.

Well, I know that the Labour meetings, the Trades and Labour meetings was where I made the breakthrough in becoming outspoken. Because when I used to attend they used to say to me, 'Any issues that you think need to be raised, you say them. Don't give it to us to say it. You say it yourself.' And, who was the one? There were a couple of fellows. Oh, Bill Timms. You probably know him.

Yes. Bill Timms would give me an urge, give me a nudge with an elbow to say things, and I was a little bit reluctant, and maybe ashamed, or a little bit reserved. But then he would give me a nudge and I would gain courage and just start asking about

Aboriginal issues. And from that time I seemed to sort of gain more confidence as I went along.

There were a lot of people with good ears but the other side was very hollow and what I said just went out the other way. Or either they were hollow on the other ear or totally deaf and they'd pretend that they were listening, but there was no action then.

Q: *Did you encounter any opposition?*

Only on the basis of ideology, I think. You know there were several ideas that you'd bring out and they said, 'Oh, no, this is not it. You'd probably do it better this way.' But there was no total objection.

Q: *Did you encounter any racism?*

Not in the trade union movement. No. We were all equal. After meetings we'd all line up to go to the bar just across the road to have a good booze up before we went home.

After the 1967 Inter-Racial Seminar I was invited to the Trades and Labour Council Christmas breaking-up party by Bill Irving. It was an all-male affair. We sat in a circle and drank enough to be pleasantly relaxed. Jokes were told to an appreciative audience. One joke was told that was 'good-natured' but extremely racist. I think the punch line referred to a 'boong' or a 'nigger' who had the biggest balls of all. Koiki took this in his stride and laughed along with the rest of the party. Indeed, when I reminded him of it he had totally forgotten the incident. It probably only stuck in my memory because I wondered how Koiki would react.

Yes. There were things like that said at times but I took it as a joke. You know, from being around with them I thought they weren't as bad as some of the people I'd seen before. *They* would totally object to the presence of a black man in their midst, in amongst the crowd, in places like pubs for instance. Or the group that I worked with on one of the rail gangs in Thiess Brothers. They wouldn't have me in the gang at all. They thought I was going to bludge on them, that they were going to do a lot more work for me. So I went away. I just went. 'Okay. That's all right.' Then I went to the next gang and joined the mixing of the concrete. And then afterwards they learned that I was doing my share of the work and their attitude changed. That was the only thing I faced at work anyway.

Afterwards, after I got involved with the Trades and Labour Council, then I realised that they [Bill Irving, Bill Timms and Fred Thompson] were members of the Communist Party. But it didn't make any difference to me because I saw them as the kind of people that I could rely on for any advice. I also went to Bonnet [then federal Liberal Member of Parliament for Herbert], but he was patronising more than giving me positive advice. And I disliked him from then on. Yes. Disliked him.

Actually [Fred Thompson, Bill Irving and Bill Timms] made me fight my own battle. They were ready to give me advice but you'd do your own battling. They were not going to stand in your way.

As I observed previously, the Communist Party had a long history of involvement with Aboriginal people. They were the first white political party to offer them support in their struggle for justice. I asked Koiki if he had ever attended Communist Party meetings.

I did. I went to a conference. There was a news crew, television, I think. The first time we had television back in 1966, I think, or '67. Or '68. I was still down the Harbour Board when we had the Inter-Racial Seminar [in 1967].

It was after that, after the Inter-Racial Seminar, that I got invited to attend a conference. I wanted to hear their State President. I believed he was a very good speaker who couldn't repeat the same word twice. And I got attracted there because I admire people who can talk on the spot in front of huge crowds of people. Anyway I went along to it. Me and Dick Hoolihan sat in the background and I really admired that man. Anyway, while he was talking, there was a camera crew working. And of course I didn't know that we were detected as well. We were picked up by the camera. And of course that night the news flash went on television and someone from the Harbour Board picked it up. And about a week later — the Vietnam War was on at that time too — someone called me a Viet Cong.

'You're a Viet Cong.'

'What are you talking about? What do you mean?'

He said, 'I saw you on television yesterday.'

Then I asked more questions.

'It was in a news flash. You were in a conference.'

I said, 'Oh yes. I went to listen to it.'

'A member of the Communist Party addressed the Conference.'

'A Communist Party conference. That's all right. It's a free country.'

But anyway it was only six months after that they transferred me from the job that I had to a sledge-hammer gang on the wharf itself. Yes, hard slugging and less money. And I said, 'That's the end of it.' And I threw it in and came out here to the university as a groundsman.

I knew Eddie Heilbronn. I knew he was a member of the Communist Party. Because where I used to live, sometimes we used to walk down town after tea, take the kids for a stroll down town. There was an almond tree between the Post Office and the Children's Services, just where the new bridge is. The Tree of

Knowledge they used to call it. And one time I walked around there and I heard him. I never ever heard of Communist people before; I never heard of them, never read anything about them. The state elections were coming up and Eddie Heilbronn somehow was a candidate, nominated himself as a candidate. He was giving a speech and I stood by and listened to it. And I picked up something. He really got me, you know. I was sort of mesmerised by the way he spoke. And I got attracted to that, and then when I saw him again down at the Harbour Board, I used to ask him a lot of questions. Because of that questioning, he suggested that I go and see Fred, Fred Thompson, about this Inter-Racial Seminar.

Fred Thompson and Bill Irving and the trade union movement were absolutely essential to the success of that conference. They did the hard work. The university people may have done a lot of the talking but the trade unions made things happen. They arranged transport for the Aboriginal people to come from Yarrabah and ensured there was adequate seating and refreshments. I asked Koiki if he had ever thought of joining the Communist Party.

No. It was like the Labor Party. I never ever joined it. I don't know why. I got nominated a couple of times, and I wanted to join the Labor Party while I was down at the Harbour Board. Then someone said, 'You've got to have a good record and no police convictions.' Well, I haven't got any police convictions anyway. They said, 'You've got to have a good record and a good police record, and you've got to know three or four members of the Labor Party who would make recommendations for you to join.' And I said, 'Oh, no. Forget it.' I didn't know any other members then. I didn't continue on with it.

Q: *Are you interested in joining any party now?*

Oh, the way things are at the moment, you know, with Katter [then the Queensland Government minister responsible for Aboriginal and Islander Affairs] saying that Aboriginal people are being prompted by people who are associated with the Labor Party, I think I am safer out of it, so that nobody could label me as being a stooge for the Labor Party.

Q: *What was it about the trade union movement that you found so important?*

I think the main thing was their interest in black affairs. That got me interested. I decided to go to Fred [Thompson] because I wanted to expand the interest of Blacks — expand the ideas. I thought if we can get assistance from them, we may be able to attract some other Blacks to join the Advancement League as well. That was the main idea. Actually, the way things went, unless you waved a dollar in front of a blackfellow, he wouldn't join you. That's what I thought. And mainly my guess wasn't too far wrong. Because as soon as Whitlam came along we started to get grants. We changed the name of the Advancement League then to Council for Indigenous People's Rights. We received our first grant of $3000 to open up an office and have a central place where people could come and get information. Then we started getting all the members. [*Laughing*] Strange.

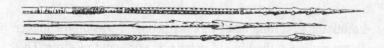

7

Netta

'She supported me all the way'

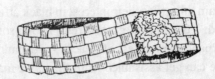

Netta had come in to Koiki's story quite a deal. I asked him to focus on the whole story again of how he came to meet Netta's people, how he came to meet Netta, and how he got married. He told the story of his first visit to The Gardens, a community of South Sea Islanders near Halifax. The South Sea Islanders had spouses of various ethnicities, and their descendants were living in self-made dwellings arranged so they could easily interact as a community and have access to the work available in the port of Lucinda and the sugarcane industry of the Ingham district.

I think the first time that I met her people, I was on the lugger *Triton* and we pulled in at Lucinda on our way to Cairns. This was to take water and some wood to boil our shells with. And I met an old Murray Islander by the name of Tonga Geesu, Cedric's uncle. And he then asked us to go to his place one afternoon. Well, that afternoon we finished work and I got a lift. I also met Kevin Saylor there. He was working on the sugar terminal. We got a lift on a truck and went to Halifax and that's where I met most of them anyway. There are several families of an old Kanaka. A fellow by the name of Jack Tanna, had married Netta's grandmother. Of course he was dead by the time I got there, but his people, his daughters, made us welcome. There were several families living there. All the daughters married into different races. One of them married a European guy. The other married a part-Aboriginal. Two of them married white guys, yes. Two married Torres Strait Islanders. And the fifth one married another Kanaka. And they were all living there. It reminded me of a Torres Strait village and the communal life was much the same as ours. And I kind of liked it because of that. And then, after we left Lucinda, we went to Cairns and I told the rest of the boys that I was leaving and we came to Innisfail. Then I came to Townsville after the incident at Innisfail where I saw my countrymen get packed up on the back of a utility by the police and taken back to Cairns. Then I decided to go canecutting and went back up there. On my way to Innisfail I heard there was a wedding on in Halifax and Netta's cousin was getting married; that was in 1958. And then I decided to go to this wedding before I joined the canecutting gang and I did. And of course Netta and I sat on the same table that night.

She was sixteen. I was about twenty, something like that. And we sat at the same table. I was dying to meet her, but in the back of my mind sort of doubted my own reasons for coming back to Halifax. I didn't know whether I was going to come back there or not, you know. It was useless for me to sort of get mixed up with someone and then have to leave and everything just falls apart. So I didn't worry about it. After the wedding I left and went to cut cane at Innisfail. Oh, the wedding at Halifax I went to was when Cedric's cousin Remon Geesu got married,[1] to Netta's cousin. So we left and went to Innisfail. And after the cane season, it was Christmas time, and a big truckload of people from Halifax had attended another wedding in Innisfail. And when I came back from the cane farm, I didn't know anybody, and I didn't realise that Netta's people were in town at the time. And, of course, I got involved with a lot of young fellows and we got pretty drunk. Right. And that wedding night, well I saw her down the street first, and I called out to her and she wouldn't come because she realised I was a bit tipsy — not a bit tipsy, I was really tipsy. And that night at the reception I asked to walk her home and she said, 'Oh, no, you are too much under the weather. You're too drunk.' And then, just as I walked out, I had a bottle of Penfolds — it's a wine, Port I think. It's nice smelling stuff. And it's pretty horrible after you get drunk on it, you know. Yes. But it leaves a nice smell in your mouth. Well, anyway, I had that tucked in my trousers and my shirt over it. Just as I walked out, this thing fell out. This bottle fell out and smashed on the cement floor. There was an old Island lady sitting there, sitting at the door, getting fresh air I think. And she started growling in Meriam Mir.

Koiki laughed softly as he remembered his embarrassment.

And I felt really small. Anyway, one of my country-ladies came out and got rid of the bottle, swept it all out. And I didn't see her [Netta] until, oh, a few months later. I just sort of thought I'd write her a letter and apologise for approaching her while I was under the influence of liquor. And that was the start of it. Because it only took about nine months after that, and we got married. I wrote her a letter and she responded and we continued writing.

I came back from Innisfail and got the same job back in the Harbour Board on the tugs and then I also got involved, when I was working at the Harbour Board, with a few of my drunken mates from the west, and so decided to go with them and try the west. I went out there and then wrote her a letter from out there. Then she asked me to come in and meet her people and I did. That was it. I was about twenty-two I think. She was seventeen. Then got married.

Koiki thought that Netta was still at school at this time but, as with his earlier confusion about the date of their wedding, he was wrong!

Her parent's reaction was quite good. All I can remember is that one of the ladies, maybe her aunty, I think, commented that she should be given another two years before she married. The way she was, just her build, anyone would think that she would have been twenty-one or twenty-two.

Netta was not Koiki's first love. He laughed at the suggestion.

Oh, no! She appeared to be different and perhaps a more homely type and I felt much more at home with her.

All of her family were very religious, all of the Tannas starting from, I think, her grandmother. Her grandmother was very religious and of course her five daughters were very religious.

The other thing about Netta is that she's not demanding. The others, they'd be hanging on to you like a blooming leech, but with her she doesn't. She doesn't do that. And of course the other thing is that she's a beautiful cook. Not that I eat very much.

I got attracted there when we were sitting around at the table and I thought, you know, it's no good getting attached to someone without being sure you were coming back here, because Halifax, you know, is a very small community, and mainly dependent on cane, and I wasn't quite sure whether I was going to cut cane for the rest of my life. So that was the reason I didn't make the initiative to meet her at the time.

I had an idea that they were very religious people and they wouldn't flirt with anyone like myself who just walked into the place. I had that in mind, but there was something else about her that I got attracted to.

I said that Netta was still very attractive.

Not so much now, old age spread I think. Middle age spread, but before, she was very attractive. And she carried herself pretty well, you know. Yes, with dignity.

I asked Koiki to tell me more about 'The Gardens', the village the South Sea Islanders built on the outskirts of Halifax. How did it remind him of a Torres Strait Islander village?

The location. The houses were located in a circle. They'd built the houses themselves. There were a lot of mangroves down the road and, of course, they provide the immediate resources for material to be used in building, mangroves. They're very strong timber, and they utilised that for building. They told me that the previous houses were shacks — grass shacks. After everybody moved out, the council turned it into a reservoir. They're not there anymore.

And the ones that had permanent jobs obtained sawn timber. Like Abraham Sailor for instance. He had a contract with the Hinchinbrook Shire Council for filling in roads with gravel that he obtained from the quarries, and he built himself a high place just on the side of the road as you turn towards Lucinda.

The houses at The Gardens were built in more or less the same style as the Torres Strait houses. Not the traditional one, the current style that we use now — you know, sort of a ridged roof and then it slopes down to a verandah, and then a floor would be anything between two to three feet off the ground. A couple of houses had a dirt floor that they eventually cemented in, cemented the floor to keep the dirt out. The houses usually had about three to four rooms and a kitchen. The bathroom was a communal one and the toilets were communal toilets.

Well, I've been going through all sorts of arguments just lately to find out what actually happened to that land. Some told me that the land was purchased by Jack Tanna and then the papers were lost somewhere along the line and none of them were able to come up with any finds, but that's what they told me. And then, somehow, there was about three generations, I think, three or four generations that lived in that area.

Q: *When were the houses cleared away by the Council?*

Oh, in '65 I would say. Yes, right until 1965.

Netta thinks that it was actually later than this. I asked Koiki if it was obvious to everyone that a Pacific Islander village existed in the Ingham district until as late as 1965.

Oh, yes. Everyone knew. White people knew. The cane farmers were very friendly to them, kind of friendly, but nobody would give them a job, mind. But there was occasional work. Whenever they needed someone, they'd grab them, but nobody was prepared to give them permanent employment. They were accepted in a way, yes. They got on quite well with the white community, yes. One of the families here that is still very friendly with us, Ganzerlas, were shopkeepers and occasionally they'd employ one of the girls from Netta's family, the two older sisters. They'd employ them as shop assistants. And they're still very friendly.

In fact they came to our twenty-fifth anniversary. They're an Italian family. She's English and he's Italian.

Koiki was not aware of any intermarriage between Torres Strait Islanders and Italians.

I think there are cases where New Australians marry into Torres Strait. We've got one girl here, Irene Akee. Her father was a German who married a Torres Strait Islander. And there are other cases, too.

Q: *Did the Pacific Islanders live together in The Gardens so that they could interact with one another?*

Yes. It was a security to be with them. You know, they had kind of emotional ties amongst the whole lot of them. I think after we got married in '59, the tenth of October '59, we started the first move of young married people moving out. There was me and Remon Geesu that moved out in the first place. See, the rest of them before us would marry and stay within the community.

I think there might have been about fifty to seventy people living there, a mixture of Torres Strait and South Sea, no problem. They identified racially as being of one stock and there's no problem in getting on with the South Sea'ers.

And when we got married, we made the first move to get out west. And when we did it, a lot of young people like Kevin Saylor also decided to come to Townsville, and then Netta's other cousin, Sunny Cassady, decided to come to Townsville as well. And eventually there were only three families left. And I think there were the Geesus. Two of Bonita's sisters married other Torres Strait Islanders. Well actually three married Torres Strait Islanders. Bonita and Rebecca and Allison married Torres Strait Islanders. And when we moved out, of course, there were only three families left. It was Dixie Gesah, and Uncle Ted and Betty, and Aunty Bet Barrett and Renny Cassady. And then in 1964, I think, or '65, Dixie and Becky moved down to Ayr and Uncle Renny Cassady bought himself a little place in Halifax itself and, of course, Ted and Betty Barrett also moved into a rented place in town in Halifax.

The Gardens was only two and a half miles from the centre of Halifax. There was no hassle at all. The Gardens was part of the community.

Some of them lived in cane barracks, you know, mainly because it was cheap to live out there in cane barracks at that time. Well, somehow they liked it.

At that time, Whites would not have rented their houses in the towns, at least, not at a price they could afford to pay.

Some of them cut cane, some of them just lived in barracks. They were scattered all over the cane farms. Those people that I'm talking about lived in a closely knitted community, lived at the village. Others were scattered in the cane barracks.

Q: *Were they canecutting or were they just living there and renting the rooms?*

They were renting them during the off season and then in the cane season they worked as cane cutters.

Q: *And they got paid full wages for that?*

Actually they got the equal pay to white cutters, whereas the Torres Strait ones that actually came from the Torres Strait to cut cane in Cairns, they were deprived of the equal wage.

Within that village, they had several ministers at times, Assembly of God. Antiknap, a fellow by the name of Antiknap. Assembly of God, yes. He was a European. There was Pastor Spoor. He was European. He stayed there at one stage. He left just before I came. He got transferred, I think. Assemblies sent him to the Atherton Tableland.

I remember when I first went to the cane field, I met an Aboriginal guy by the name of George Davis. He now lives in Atherton and the Pastor arranged with George to come down and pick us up to go to his church on the Pinnacle Pocket near Yungaburra. It didn't work out. But instead I went to another little community of both Aboriginals and South Sea Islanders at Little Mulgrave. One Sunday I just spent the whole day with them. And that's where I met Georgy Davis.

In The Gardens the church was centred right in the middle and all the houses were built around the church. Right in the centre of it. And there was a communal well that old Jack Tanna dug. And there was a water tank on top, and they built it themselves. They got wood from somewhere and put a tank up on top and ran the pipes themselves to reach the houses.

Koiki's knowledge of The Gardens' history was a little astray. Netta informed me that Jack Tanna did not dig the well. Renny Cassady divined the well and Netta's uncles dug it.

The Gardens was a remarkable creation attesting to the strength of Australia's South Sea Islander people and to the Torres Strait Islander spouses and those of other ethnic groups who came to share their life. I asked Koiki if he had ever seen other villages in mainland Australia like it. Perhaps the one at Little Mulgrave.

No. That's the only one I'd seen. This community [at Little Mulgrave, near Cairns] was scattered all over the cane fields and all over the cane barracks. All over the place. It wasn't a living together sort of thing. But they came together to one of the fellow's place — I can't remember his name at the moment. I know he looked like a Torres Strait Islander. They came to his place on the side of the Mulgrave River and on Sundays they used to have church there and then have a picnic lunch and then have afternoon service before everybody went home. I think there were round about thirty to forty people. They were all Assemblies of God. Actually my brother's wife came from that group, in the same group that used to assemble.

They were a mixture. They were a mixed group. Some were Aboriginals. Georgy Davis, for instance, is an Aboriginal, and his wife is a Kanaka and my brother's wife, Nicey's wife, is a Kanaka.[2] Right. And they used to come together from Mulgrave, from Yungaburra sometimes. Or sometimes this lot [from The Gardens] would travel up there to Yungaburra and congregate in the church at Pinnacle Pocket. Some of them worked for cane farmers. They were employed by the local cane farmers.

Others were living in the barracks, paying rent. One reason was cheap accommodation and this white attitude towards Blacks. You know, won't let them into the town itself. They were let in only after the Commonwealth made money available for the State to purchase houses in town for the black people. That was in the '60s. I think after that Inter-Racial seminar that we conducted in 1967.

After we had the seminar it took twelve months for Minister Wentworth to make up his mind to give the money to the State specifically for that purpose [for housing]. Because he came to our seminar and addressed us, and it took him twelve months before he did that. And that was the time that we were so called 'let in' to live in the little town areas like Halifax.

With deliberate irony, Koiki used the term 'let in' to echo the process used in Queensland in the nineteenth century of 'keeping the Blacks out' and 'letting the Blacks in'. Aborigines were driven away from any areas needed by the settlers by the use of the Native Police or settler vigilantes. When their resistance was broken and they were thought to be no longer a danger or an obstruction to settler activities, they were 'let in' as a controlled inferior caste. This process had been a topic in my Australian race relations course that Koiki attended.

Q: *Were there other ways that The Gardens reminded you of a Torres Strait Islander village?*

The people's behaviour, the way they interacted between each other. Netta's mum also reminded me of my mum. Netta's mum was also a small woman, an asthmatic. I felt very much at home there. And when they knew I was coming, they would go out fishing. They would do all sorts of other things for me. Treated me like a king. I got attracted to them.

I don't know what it was, but they treated me like a king. Her dad, the old fella, he would go out after crabs because he knew I loved seafood and he'd go out and get them for me, and if he knew I was coming on the weekend, he'd have them there. And he also knew that I loved fruit and he'd have cases of fruit for me to take back out west.

Most of the people at The Gardens, men and women, worshipped regularly with white pastors in the Assembly of God Church, but not all.

Well, there was Netta's dad and uncle Renny Cassady. They would go to church when they feel like it, but most of the time either they're out in the cane field or they're out in the mud flats somewhere, either fishing or looking for crabs or gone hunting somewhere. But they weren't as good Christians as their wives were. The majority of them went to church. Only those two men that I know were outlaws.

Koiki chuckled at his depiction of his old friends.

The church had an accommodation at the back for the white pastor. They [the Islanders and the pastor] built it themselves. Jack Tanna built the first church for the Assembly.

This, the first of the churches of The Gardens, was built of grass. The Torres Strait Islanders had all been Anglican in the Torres Strait.

They switched across mainly because that was the only church with the majority of their own people in it, their wives' people. And they went to the Assemblies then. There was some belief too, that Torres Strait Islanders had, that Pentecostal churches were better religion than the Anglicans. They were more powerful because of that talking in tongues and all that. We don't experience that in the Anglican Church at all; there it's all formally written up. It's all formal, right, whereas in the Assemblies it's free movements.

There was more spiritual power in the Assembly of God Church than there was in the Anglican Church. One reason was that they talk in tongues and the other was that they had healing power. And they also had rules in terms of restricting its members from drinking habits, from smoking, and from running around stupid in town and all that kind of stuff. It became part of their life. And they lived, more or less, to their religion, to that.

Netta, you know, grew up in it and it probably took me about fifteen years to get my influence across to her [*Laughing*]. My influence was that we should remain neutral and go to either church, because, after all, we're all looking at the same thing. Worshipping the same thing.

I never went to church when Netta was going to church at the village. When I first went to Halifax, there was no pastor there. They used to have one or two services a week. And it didn't happen on a weekend I was there.

I went to one of their church services when Eddie, our first boy, got dedicated, and it was at the Methodist Church because they didn't have the pastor then at the Gardens. Dedication is like a baptism in the Anglican church. Then they do baptise them afterwards. There's two processes, I think. In the Anglican you've got the baptism and the confirmation. So I went to that and to me it looked like an Anglican baptism.

Apparently Eddie was the only child that I had dedicated in a church. Well, Netta has much the same opinion as I have now. We feel now that we don't want to impose our values on the kids, our beliefs on kids. They will find out for themselves.

Koiki didn't think that Netta missed her contact with the church. I asked Koiki how important Netta had been in his life.

Well, from within the struggle itself, right, apart from our own personal lives, she's able to hang on to money. That's one thing. And that way we were able to save when we were out west. We were both working out west. She was cooking at the station and I was on the navvying gang before the first kid came. And we were able to save some money to put a deposit on a house.

She's able to hold on to money and she also restricted me from spending. [*We both laughed.*] And she, more or less, had a stranglehold on me. Before, I used to just get it, send some to my mum and the rest I'd go into town and either play it on the billiard table or drink it all or give it away to somebody. And when we got married, she was able to hang on to it. Then, apart from that, she also became aware of the problems that we were facing in terms of discrimination. Several times we brought our kids in to Hughenden when they were sick and the doctor would see them — Eddie and Maria for instance, when they were babies, when we were out west. And we couldn't get a lift. We didn't have a vehicle at that time. Only very few people had them and we didn't. And there was no way of getting back so we had to go to the nearest pub, or whatever, and ask for a room; and for all the times that we used to come in, *all* of the pubs didn't take us. They wouldn't accept black money, or probably they thought we'd leave our skin on the sheets.

Even through winter, you know how cold it gets out there, and even through winter we would sleep at the railway station on the platform with the two kids. And because of that I thought something would have to be done. We'd have to get political. And then, I think the starting point of my getting involved in it was that I used to listen to Longreach radio sometimes. I was, you know, politically minded when I left the Islands, but I didn't know the art of organising a group of people together. And I used to listen to Longreach radio sometimes and I think there was a talkback or whatever program, something like the community input programs, and occasionally Joe McGuinness would come on and Kath Walker, and I started to admire those two people. Then I started organising the gangs on the railway line to come together as an organisation so that we don't get shoved around on the railway lines like they were doing. And then I found the mob rather difficult to organise because we didn't come together to start off with as a common thing.

We Torres Strait Islanders were too busy trying to get acquainted with the whole surroundings then. We were all new to the area. Then after a while I was stuck up several times in Hughenden and kicked up a hell of a stink and caused physical fights at times, with white guys, publicans and all them. And that was the only time, whenever that sort of thing happened, we all came together. And then, after, we organised this strike in the camps of the Hornibrooks when the police went there with guns and were kicking out all the ringleaders. Police from Hughenden anyway went to Prairie with guns to get rid of the ringleaders of that strike. And then after that Netta was getting familiar with what I was on about, because I used to talk to her about independent schools and all that sort of thing.

We decided to come to Townsville then because Eddie was about three years old then, I think. When we came to Townsville we lived in a flat for two years while we were paying off our block of land. I mentioned earlier I think that we went for a walk down Flinders Street and listened to some of the people who were talking (I think it was election time). I heard several speakers and Eddie Heilbronn, a member of the Communist Party, got up and spoke, and I took an interest in his speech. Then after a while I joined the Art Society, the Townsville Art Society, just some place where we could go to at night. And then one night the Art Society put on an exhibition and attracted quite a lot of people and Dick Hoolihan was amongst them. And he came around and he started talking to me about what I was doing. One thing we had in common, we both heard Kath Walker and Joe McGuinness on radios at times and we started discussing them, discussing Joe McGuinness and Kath. Then eventually we decided that we should have some sort of organisation, and in '63, I think, '63 or '64 (I'm not quite sure now), we decided that the Advancement League was a way out. Then we got together. There were several people that we invited to come. Dick knew them, you see — Fred Thompson, Frank Bishop, Charlie (a fella by the name of Charlie; I can't remember his name; he was a meatworker), and several members of the Labor Party. They were mainly old fellas, anyway. And I think Fred and I were the youngest ones there, Fred Thompson and myself. I was the very youngest and Fred, of course, is a lot older than I am. We had the first meeting and me and Dick became the President and the Secretary of the Advancement League. Dick occupied the position of the Secretary/Treasurer. He was a mean old man too.

*We both laughed at this vision of our old friend determinedly
controlling the purse strings.*

Yes, with money he was very mean. Yes. We became the President and Secretary/Treasurer of the Advancement League, Townsville Branch.

You know, I mentioned I was cutting cane up at Gordonvale. I met a fellow by the name of Saveka, George Saveka. He was a cane farmer, too, a Torres Strait Islander. He was the only Torres Strait Islander I know who was a successful cane farmer. He is now an Anglican priest. And there was another guy, another old man by the name of Joseph. He was a Meriam man. I met them in Cairns one time and they told me about the Advancement League and I went to one of the meetings. I met Joe McGuinness there, Joe and Amy. When I came to Townsville, I met Dick and we thought, right, we'll get ourselves together, get ourselves organised and invite either Kath Walker or Joe to come here and address us to form up the first advisory committee in Townsville.

And we did it with the help of the Trades and Labour Council. They gave us some money. I think, it was just enough for the rail fares and we paid Joe's way and he came down and addressed the conference. And during that time a lot of Aboriginal people used to live at Stuart in the gun shelters and all around that area there. They were Josephine Sailor and all the others.

*I commented that I found it hard to imagine Josephine Sailor
living with a group of fringe dwellers in old World War II gun
emplacements.*

That's where she used to live, at Stuart, and all her sisters, their mother and the old fellow. They all used to. Josephine's father, old man Baker, was a mate, a countryman of Dick Hoolihan's. He was Dick Hoolihan's countryman from the Valley of

Lagoons. That's where they come from. They were born in the caves up there.

While this was developing, Netta's attitude was much the same as the church-influenced people. I learnt at that time the difference between the Communist Party and the Labor Party and the Liberals and the Country Party and that Queensland was governed by a coalition of both the Liberals and the National Party, the Country Party.

And because she was constantly being brainwashed, maybe during her childhood days, against Communism — either through the Church or somewhere along the line anyway — she developed a very bad attitude towards them, towards Communists. And she threatened me at one stage. She said, 'If you don't get out of it, I'm going to leave'. I had to get out of the Advancement League and all the organisations that I was getting involved in, or she was going to leave. And then I tried my hardest and then eventually I convinced her that we've got no one to turn to. The moderate political organisations won't listen to our pleas. We've got to have white support. You know, we're very much in need of it and we should grab any hand that comes to us. And she eventually took it in and said welcome to people like Fred Thompson and Frank Bishop. They would come in at any time and she would welcome them. I eventually convinced her. Not only them, there were a lot of Labor people that I was friendly with. They would also come too.

And we developed a kind of link between the Blacks and the Labor movement as a whole. The other thing that made it easier was that I used to take her, sometimes, to a Trades and Labour meeting where we wouldn't be hearing from one particular group, but a whole spectrum of the Labor movement.

I suggested to Koiki that it must have been a long step for Netta

from her Islander village outside Halifax, which itself was a
backwater village near Ingham, to becoming aware of the
political complexities of the world.

Yes. That's right. Even for me too it was a big step from that little
island in the Strait.

What I mean is that, when I grew up, there was no state-wide
politics being discussed anywhere in the Islands, except the
Island politics alone, but I think I sort of grew beyond that. I
started looking at Torres Strait Islanders as a whole and why the
whole range of Islanders were exploited as cheap labour in the
pearling industry. And I started to question that within my own
mind. And the other thing that worried me was the limited
education that was made available to us in the Torres Strait. Well,
one of the things that hit me was that if the schools were run by
my parents, I was certain that they would look for the best people
to teach us, but because it was handled by someone else, we
could only get whatever that someone else was offering. I was
sixteen years old on Murray when I came to that conclusion.

Q: *What made you think that the education you were getting was*
not a good one?

Well, I actually experienced it myself when I came to TI. See
Blacks were segregated in one school at a place called Ling's
Camp and the other school was situated for the Whites on Green
Hills.

I was told that the white school had offered much more in
terms of the study of science, for instance. There was more taught
in social studies; there was more taught in geography and all that
kind of stuff. There was nothing like that happening to us. All
we were learning was to read and write. We didn't even study
our own history.

No, there was nothing like that taught, not even our own

culture. There were no dances, there was no weaving, or no artefacts, no handicraft, there was nothing like that taught. Nothing at all. That is what made me think that maybe if I was a captain in the ship, I would direct it in a different direction. And when I came to Townsville, this idea came into being, after I met all these different people.

I asked Koiki how Netta reacted to the various adventurous, even controversial, schemes he proposed.

Well, one thing about it, she supported me all the way, apart from the initial objection to the members of the Labor and Communist Parties coming to my house. After she got over that hurdle, she then became very supportive in whatever schemes I was involved in. She was there all the time; and I could rely on her to help me prepare towards whatever we were doing. The other thing that makes her different was that if I had, say, married a European or one of my own people, I think I wouldn't have grown to the stages I did politically — maybe because I was able to discuss things with her, talk with her, even though she doesn't get carried away the way I do. But she is able to give me a hearing.

She listens to me. She does at times give me her point of view. She pulls me up and says, 'Look, I think this is a bit wrong there. You better go back and do a bit more thinking before you do it.' But in my opinion it is not enough sometimes. I hoped that she would really push me to stop and think.

Well, I think it's a normal woman's reaction, that woman's love can only stem from man's want. That's what I think anyway.

He laughed good-naturedly at his very Torres Strait Islander, male view of life.

That's my theory. I think she was attracted to me initially, but over the years I have been trying to question her about that but she hasn't told me. Maybe she doesn't want to let me know how she felt. But when I first met her, after I had been out west and back, she didn't want to part with me again. And we just sort of hit it off from there on.

In his various endeavours, Koiki had become involved with a number of white men and women who were willing to support him, but, in my mind, some women had been remarkably committed. I asked him which women had been most important in his struggle.

I think most of them, the ones that we mentioned like Patsy Brown, Sandra Renew, Julia Koppe, Lyn Henderson, were important to me. They're important because I can rely on them for advice for whatever problems I've got and I can go to them and say, 'Look, how do I go about this?' And men, just the same. But with the ones that were immediately close to me, say around Townsville, I never had any kind of relationship with them apart from being a good friend. Anwyl Burfein and Sandra were the most important to me.

I treated them as sisters, as my sisters, and they also had the same sort of attitude towards me. You know we were all so close, mainly because I think Rob Renew, Sandra's brother, was like that. He was like my brother to me. We did all sorts of things at the school. Rob Renew was the first teacher there. He lasted for about a term to get us off the ground. Anwyl was there at the same time.

Q: *In what way were Sandra and Anwyl especially valuable?*

Well, in all the things that go with the school; for instance I would call on them and ask them for what sort of reaction I would get if I did this; and what sort of reaction I would get from the education authorities. And what would happen if we were to introduce, say, the language course that Julia helped to develop, Van Leer, all that sort of thing? And of course the Education Act: they would read it and try and explain it to me. I'd read it but I'd want to make sure that someone else would explain it so that I could get it clear in my mind. How to tackle it if a problem arises? And for the legal side of schooling, you know, I would rely on them. And Doug Turnbull from the Legal Service was also very helpful in that case. Doug, of course, came in later.

I think I find both men and women easy people to approach, like Geoff Coombs, in the education field. I find him easy to talk to and he finds it the same way with me and we get on quite well. And even, you know, yourself. We are able to get on quite well. And with women, I think, mainly because we were dealing with primary kids. The women, you know, maybe because of their maternal make-up, understand primary kids much more than a man teacher would. And that's why I turned to them for advice.

These women and others seemed to become committed to you and your projects. Some worked for very little money or almost nothing to keep the school afloat and they didn't place making a career for themselves as the highest priority in their lives.

Yes, I know I have sort of demanded a lot and placed more work on them, but I don't think they minded at all. There was a lot of sacrifice from their side and I really appreciated that. And I don't think I'd get it if I did go into it again. I've still got my doubts whether I am going to get people like that again.

You know they are idealists as well. I know some other organisations where they placed white people in it and the Whites made sure that they obtained full wages out of it, whereas there was nothing like that at all. I think the people that worked also realised that we didn't have any money to offer them.

And they wouldn't accept any money I think if I did offer it. But if we'd have made a go of it, I think they would have accepted it in the end. But in the initial stages there was not enough to provide that. Actually I also suffered myself, you know, because while I was gardening at the university, when Anwyl got there, part of my wages from gardening was going into her and Rob's pay — to meet their rent anyway.

Q: *Why did you give up working at the university as a gardener?*

Well, there were two things. One was that Rob was leaving. Right. Rob had to leave and get a job somewhere else where he earned himself a normal wage. And then a man's influence was needed in that school because we were dealing with kids who came from different areas, different areas of the Torres Strait and with different kinds of behavioural patterns; and you needed a man there to be able to control that. I had to be there. And I did it for no wages at all, same as the others, for a long time. Netta was working as a teacher-aide with Anwyl and I think she received more or less three days' wage. So was Anwyl as well. They only got paid for two or three days and the rest of the time was devoted free. And we lived on that wage for a very long time until, I think, up to 1977.

I think the best wage I've ever earned was when I got employed by the Commonwealth Employment Service as a temporary vocational officer. I was there for three years, three and a half years. Actually I left it because I couldn't understand their mentality, the manager's mentality, in trying to promote Aboriginal employment and yet they weren't making any resources available for people like myself to use in terms of promoting Aboriginal employment, such as time allowed for the interview of employers, and use of a vehicle to canvass positions. That sort of thing. And the other thing was that he was accepting reports that never happened from other officers. They were lodging reports: someone went out on behalf of the Aboriginal Employment and Training Branch and interviewed such and such. And when I did the follow-up, the employers would tell me that nobody had been there, and that got me. Why put in a report when that kind of thing never eventuated?

Q: *Why did they put in that sort of report?*

Just to make themselves look busy.

Q: *What would they have done instead of doing that?*

I don't know. Brian McLoud and myself did the research on the reports and followed up where these reports came from and the employers' names that were quoted in those reports, and we found that these employers were never ever interviewed at all.

Mabo said that the staff's reaction to his allegations was another reason for his leaving the CES.

I was threatened to get my head bashed in if I ever did that again. Or there was going to be an accident in the office. There was a group of them, the staff members. One of them came and seen me but I know there were about four or five others. Well, they were involved in the report writing as well.

The only way out was to leave the place. They had other black people who didn't mind that sort of thing happening in the office. I'm not going to do that kind of shit. If I want to get a job done, I'll get it done. I'm not going to put in false reports.

And the other thing that upset me, what really upset me, was that over the years that we've been in Townsville, there was no Torres Strait Island apprentice until I went there. And I was trying my hardest to get Torres Strait apprentices in. I wasn't given the use of the vehicle to do that kind of work. That's what disappointed me. And there were three apprentices after I left.

Apart from the time he had to walk for forty kilometres from Townsville along the railway line looking for work in a railway gang, in his early years Koiki Mabo seemed to be able to find employment rather easily. He threw his job in a number of times to try something else or, as in the above case, on principle. For some of the time that he was involved in the Murray Island land claim he could not find employment. Sometimes he could not seek paid employment because of the necessity of visiting Murray Island and other places for extensive periods of time. Indeed I stopped recording his life story because I was never sure when he would be in Townsville. And of course neither of us expected his sudden death.

I asked Koiki how Netta reacted when he told her he was going to throw in a job.

She worried. She worried and there was nothing she could do. It was me that was confronting it most of the time. While I was at the CES she continued to work for the school, the Black Community School. She was also earning a teacher-aide wage and that sort of kept us afloat because we didn't have anything else to worry about, except rates and maintenance on the house, because we had paid that off before I left the university out of my gardening wages.

Q: *It wasn't bought by the Communist Party as someone once said?*

Oh, no. *[We both laughed.]*

The land in those days, when we were out west, was going out for about £600 and we bought about three blocks when we were out west. As I said, Netta became very tight in terms of holding on to money. The two of us worked. She worked at the station cooking and I was on the railway line and she use to ride her bike across. It was only about a mile away from where we were anyway. And that is where we sort of saved some money.

I think we both agreed initially, we made an agreement, that we would take care of our money and try and make the best of it and buy ourselves a house so that we can rear up a family in our own place. And then when we came to Townsville, I was still paying the land off when I was at the Harbour Board. And, of course, I had a good job there. I use to clear about £120 a week. It was big money in those days, especially during the cane season when the ships used to come in at any time. They used to wake me up and take me out to the Harbour and I'd stay up all night and then start work again next morning at 8 o'clock. And of course we paid the land off. The other thing that happened in my favour was that my uncle had an accident out west, Kebisu Fred. His name was Kebisu Fred. He had an accident out west and he came to the hospital here and I brought him home. He had no one to go to after he got let out as an outpatient and I thought, oh well, I am the nearest relative here, I will take him, so we took him. And then one night we sat around and I asked him questions. How did the accident happen? He didn't want to tell me because the fellow that he was with told him not to tell the police what had happened. And I asked him and he told me. And I said, 'Oh, you've got a case for third party insurance anyway.' I took him to John Bolton from Nehmer and Bolton, Solicitors, and explained the case to him and he said, 'Oh, yes, you've got a good case to claim third party insurance.' And he did. And he got $30,000 and out of that he gave me $1500 to pay the rest of my bills off the land. $1,500 was the amount owing on the land, the three blocks that I owned. Actually we came from the same tribe, from my grandmother's side, and my grandmother and his grandfather were brothers and sisters.

PART III

The final years

8

A very active activist

'A big step from that little island'

In 1981, at a conference in Townsville hosted by the Townsville Treaty Committee (Mabo and I were co-chairmen) and the James Cook University Students Union, a group of Murray Islanders decided to mount a challenge in the High Court to reclaim their land rights. The case, *Eddie Mabo and Others v. The State of Queensland*, commenced in the High Court of Australia in May 1982. A preliminary hearing in October 1982 failed to reach an agreed statement of facts. In 1985 the Queensland Government passed the Queensland Coast Islands Declaratory Act to extinguish retrospectively any native title that may have existed prior to the annexation of the outer Torres Strait Islands in 1879. In February 1987 the Supreme Court of Queensland commenced proceedings, at the request of the High Court, to determine issues of fact in the Meriam case, Justice Moynihan presiding. These proceedings were adjourned when the legal counsel for the

Meriam plaintiffs launched a challenge in the High Court to the validity of the Queensland Coast Islands Declaratory Act. In December 1988, by a majority of four to three, the High Court declared the Queensland Act invalid because it conflicted with the 1975 Commonwealth Racial Discrimination Act. The Supreme Court of Queensland recommenced proceedings in 1989. Justice Moynihan delivered his judgement on 16 November 1990 and acknowledged that Murray Islanders had a system of land ownership before 1879 which he believed still existed. However, he explicitly excluded Mabo's claims and declared him an unreliable witness. (This was discussed in Chapter 1.)

In May 1991 *Eddie Mabo and Others v. The State of Queensland* was recommenced in the High Court, and on 3 June 1992 the decision was handed down in favour of the plaintiffs by a majority of six to one. The High Court acknowledged that native title had existed on Murray Island and throughout Australia since time immemorial. The concept of *terra nullius* on which Australia was founded had been rejected. During these ten years three of the claimants, Sam Passi, Celuia Salee and Koiki Mabo, died. The other two, the Rev. Dave Passi and James Rice, still reside on Murray Island.

Since my last recorded interview with Koiki Mabo in November 1984, I have read his diaries and personal papers and talked with some members of his family, especially his wife, Bonita, and his daughter Maleta. The picture that emerges, even apart from his involvement with the consultations and legal proceedings associated with the various court hearings, is that of an extraordinarily active, rich and turbulent life. Because he belonged to a number of committees, he had a regular round of meetings to attend with their resultant work and human involvement. There were also community meetings to discuss pressing issues and the essential but time-consuming interaction with countrymen, relatives and friends.

From June 1981 to December 1984, Koiki had been a student teacher at James Cook University hoping that a course in education would prepare him for a more meaningful involvement with the Black Community School. Classroom teaching, however, was not for him, especially when he found himself teaching infant classes. He had entered tertiary education too old to take on such a role, one that he found almost an affront to his male Torres Strait Islander dignity. On a number of occasions during his last years, he considered re-enrolling in university courses. Indeed, he had a discussion with Donald Whaleboat about this less than three months before he died. He had already received a grant from the Australian Institute of Aboriginal Studies in 1985 to research Torres Strait Islander land tenure, and he believed no one had more knowledge of Torres Strait Islander culture than he. Anthropology was the discipline that now attracted him.[1]

From 1985 to 1988 Koiki had three challenging and creative jobs. In 1985 he was a Field Officer with the Townsville Aboriginal and Islander Legal Service. This involved liaising with the police, the prison and the Aboriginal and Islander people caught up in the legal process. His diary reveals a dutiful concern for his official duties, but inevitably Koiki grafted on a socio-political dimension which involved his interacting more broadly with community members. From my perspective, he seemed to have made it into a very creative position. However, before the end of the year, there was friction with the local Aboriginal Manager who believed that Koiki was spending too much time on community work. So four years into the native title challenge, Mabo was once again unemployed.

In 1986 Koiki became Assistant Director, Aboriginal Arts, at the Melbourne Moomba Festival. He maintained with pride that he was responsible for the first Aboriginal participation in Moomba. This was a good preparation for his subsequent position as Community Arts Officer working for the Department of Aboriginal Affairs in Townsville. In this role he was heavily involved in the planning and organisation of the fifth Festival of Pacific Arts held in Townsville in August 1988. This position terminated after the Festival and Koiki was unemployed for the remaining three years of his life.[2]

During the whole time I knew Mabo he was always bubbling with some new idea, some scheme he was trying to get off the ground or to develop further. Indeed I first met him as a result of one of these imaginative leaps: the Inter-Racial Seminar held in Townsville in 1967. We got to know each other over the months of meetings and preparation. I attended the Trades and Labour Council Christmas party where we met again and I invited him to join me at the Christmas breaking-up party of the Townsville High School staff at the local pub, an all-male affair. In those days, only a few desperately lonely or outrageously conscientious students turned up on the last day of school and they soon drifted off.

I had forgotten my invitation to Koiki and was surprised when he walked in after work, in time for the last round or two of drinks. He joined this surprised group of white school teachers, all of us much the worse for wear by this time, and seemed as comfortable as if we were all Islanders. When we were leaving, one of my senior colleagues growled at me as we headed off to our cars, 'That was a mongrel act'.

I have never understood why he found my invitation to a Torres Strait Islander to join us for a drink as 'a mongrel act', and when I discussed it with him recently, he had totally forgotten the incident. He wasn't and isn't racist and it had occurred thirty years ago. He probably thought I had put Koiki into an embarrassing situation. Neither of us was embarrassed, partly because of our months of meetings. But we had both previously had a good deal of casual cross-cultural experience, as it would be termed today, Koiki in his work and through the trade unions, and me at Quamby, in a one-teacher school north of Cloncurry in western Queensland. Here I had taught Aboriginal children, socialised with their families and friends, and drunk with the local men and the pastoral workers from the district when they came into the Quamby Pub, as well as with the station owners, managers and white ringers for whom Quamby, population forty, was the local club. There was a clear if informal caste system, based on race, class and gender, but as the local, transient schoolie, I could move easily through the barriers. I was there for almost two years, twenty years old when I arrived, and it was the first meaningful contact I had had with Aboriginal people. I even bought Elkin's classic with its now embarrassing title, *The Australian Aborigines: How to Understand Them*, and soon discovered that the people I was meeting were very different from the ones he described. They were more like the people I would meet at the Inter-Racial Seminar in Townsville in 1967. There were very few Aborigines at Quamby from remote Aboriginal reserves and missions who were 'under the Act', sent out to work on stations as cheap black labour, and prevented from controlling their own earnings, drinking alcohol and travelling or marrying without permission. I only got to know one, the 'black boy' rouseabout at the pub, Freddie, who slept in his swag on the cement floor in the laundry and worked on the publican's station when needed. It was 1955. So in 1967 when I invited Koiki for a drink it never occurred to me that it was a mongrel act. The fact that my friend did says a lot about the Townsville of 1967.

The Inter-Racial Seminar was Mabo's idea. The National Party Government thought it was 'a mongrel act' and subjected the organisers to police scrutiny. We were certain our phones were tapped and the local clergy were warned not to involve themselves in this Communist-front activity. Many ignored the advice.

When Mabo and Burnum Burnum, whom we knew then as Harry Penrith, started the Black Community School in 1973, the *Townsville Daily Bulletin* and some senior education administrators thought that was a mongrel act and did their best to destroy it at birth. They failed. The idea burned on for twelve years because of Mabo's dedication.

In Townsville in the late 1970s a group of Torres Strait Islanders, among them Koiki Mabo and Seriana Tapim, suggested that one organisation be formed to represent all of Townsville's Islander population. As a result *Magani Malu Kes* was formed. *Magani* in the Western, Central and Eastern Islands means Torres Strait. *Malu* is Western Island for 'deep water', and *Kes*, is Eastern Island for 'passage' or 'strait'. Thus the name symbolically incorporated the three island groupings. *Magani Malu Kes* continues to be an important organisation for the large Torres Strait Islander community in Townsville.[3]

In August 1978 Mabo presented on behalf of the Black Community School a successful funding proposal to the Australian Institute of Aboriginal Studies to enable him to explore the possibility of the establishment of the Magani Institute. This was a wide-ranging proposal concerned primarily with matters of educational and cultural significance. Mabo suggested it become the parent organisation for the Black Community School and other such Torres Strait Islander schools which Mabo envisaged developing in the near future at Mackay and even on Murray Island, although each school would be run by a Parents Council.

Typically, Mabo proposed 'that the Magani Institute shall consider the possible erection of a school at Dam, near Las, on the site of the place of the traditional education of the youth of Mer'.[4] The proposal was a rejection of the education provided for Islanders by the Queensland Government. The inclusion of Mer made this especially clear as there was already a state school there for the Meriam people, Mabo being one of its graduates.

Mabo highlighted a number of areas of concern for the Magani Institute. Not surprisingly, the mastery of English was a top priority. On behalf of the Black Community School, he wrote:

> We propose that the need for special attention to the needs of Torres Strait Islander children learning English in schools in Australia be extensively studied by the Magani Institute, and that the Magani Institute provide expertise for other community groups seeking solutions to the general problems of English literacy among Torres Strait Islander children.

One section entitled 'Curriculum' indicated how:

> the Magani Institute shall develop curricular materials for use in teaching traditional languages and culture, both within constituent schools and in other schools where learning about Torres Strait Islanders is desired.

The mastery of English was to be assisted by the development of resources to teach English as a second language to Torres Strait children and adults, using Torres Strait Islander Creole, *Brokan*, as the language of instruction:

> [*Brokan* is] the *lingua franca* of the Strait and ... the primary language of most of the Torres Strait Islander children. It is also the principal language of several Torres Strait Islander communities, and of many of the Torres Strait Islanders now living in Australia.

There were a number of services listed for the Magani Institute to provide: educational consultation, an information centre about all things Torres Strait Islander, a translation service, an information service for Islanders about white Australian culture (*kolé ra tonar*), a community service linking government agencies and Torres Strait Islander people, a Magani Institute housing fund, administered by the community services section to ensure all Islanders were provided with adequate housing, and a Magani Institute research centre to conduct or contract research needed by government agencies and other bodies.

A substantial part of the proposal dealt with 'cultural studies' under the headings: academic research, sacred sites, traditional ownership, genealogy, and cultural materials. Mabo's proposal aimed at researching, describing, restoring and maintaining traditional and contemporary Torres Strait Islander culture as well as promoting commercial opportunities for Torres Strait Islander creativity.

The proposal for the establishment of the Magani Institute is imaginative and challenging even in 1996, and worthy of further consideration. Seen in the context of 1978 it is quite extraordinary. The Bjelke-Petersen Government was in power. It had just defied the Fraser Coalition Government in Canberra over outstations and increased autonomy for Aboriginal people on Mornington Island and Aurukun, and there seemed no prospect for land rights in Queensland. Yet from the small group of people associated with the Black Community School, this proposal was drafted. Once again Mabo and his supporters were years ahead of their time and the seed fell upon stony ground.

Mabo's other successful application for funding to the Australian Institute of Aboriginal Studies was submitted in November 1984. It was focused on recording the traditional boundaries determining land ownership on Murray Island and the sacred sites, especially those associated with the Malo-Bomai cult. The Magani Institute proposal was obviously worked over at great

length, typed and presented with a cool, academic professional-
ism. The 1984 proposal is rushed and handwritten in order to get
the funding so that Mabo could work through January and
February 1985 while he was on his university vacation. During
this time there was to be a tombstone unveiling which would
bring many Islanders back to Mer whom Mabo could consult.
He was also trying to accomplish as much as possible before the
Services legislation accompanying the Queensland Deeds of
Grant in Trust legislation came into operation. Moreover, the
mapping of traditional boundaries would be important in the
Native Title High Court challenge and would provide him with
a wonderful opportunity to discuss all of these matters with the
Murray Islanders. In the extracts below, Mabo's determination
that young Torres Strait Islanders and future generations would
know their inheritance is poignantly expressed.

The aim of this Project is to carry out the recording of Traditional
Boundaries of
1. Tribal Areas
2. Clan land
3. Individual or family land
4. Sacred sites
5. Restoration of Shrines and Zogos of each Tribe & clan groups.

Traditionally in the Torres Strait land has been owned & occupied
quite differently from the land ownership by the Aboriginal people
on the mainland. Therefore it would be necessary to carry out this
project in several sequences; for instance, stage one would be to
hold a public meeting and inform the Public of Mer the reasons for
such project to be undertaken and ask for their cooperation.

No such recordings has ever been done at all. It is most important
that this type of Recording be done at this Stage before the New Qld
Govt's Services Legislation takes its full effect, and it would be
disastrous if none of this type of information is passed on to our
future generations.

This type of information would also be of help to young Islanders
Born on the mainland through no fault of their own. This generation

having no first hand experiences of Mer (Is) would no doubt find themselves in a difficult position of identifying themselves with their particular land. Recording of such land can also become a useful Resource material for use in Schools and Colleges. It has become necessary that we as Islanders carry out these projects ourselves, because we feel the Torres Strait Area and its people are of No Acamedic interest to Professional Researchers. Therefore large institutions on the mainland hold very little informations about our people and their culture.

This Project will enable me to document boundaries and Sacred Sites of Malo-Bomai Cult of Mer. It will be very beneficial to the people of Mer. As stated earlier such boundries will be forgotten in the next 20 years or so because of the New Qld Act and the Transmigration of Islanders to the North Qld Cities on the Mainland Qld. This could be the start of a major project which could spread across the whole of the Strait. We have some Islanders in Townsville who have been here for 30 years & their descendants have no knowledge of their traditional lands. It is important for these youngsters to understand their traditional heritage before it is lost forever.

My reference to this 'exciting and important proposal' is also handwritten and rushed. The extract below catches some of the urgency:

I have known Mr Mabo very well since 1967 when we were both involved in the Inter-Racial Seminar held in Townsville: 'We the Australians: What Is to Follow the Referendum?' During this time Mr Mabo has shown an unshakable commitment to fostering the survival and growth of his Torres Strait Islander culture in the changed circumstances of the present and future. His development & implementation of the concept of the Black Community School in Townsville over so many years is proof of this, in part, if proof is needed. Mr Mabo has been a student of mine this semester. During this time he has recorded the history of the Mabo clan and has been appointed my part-time research assistant to flesh out that history.[5]

In retrospect, these seem exciting times in which I was to some extent a fringe dweller of the historic process Koiki was engaged upon. But this is with the benefit of hindsight. The historic High Court decision was then at best an enticing mirage. The excitement was in being caught up with Mabo's imagination and drive.

During his final years he was still actively developing long-range plans, one of the most ambitious being Mer Island Fisheries, also known as Meriam Trading Company Ltd. This company was incorporated under the Queensland Companies Act by Richard Doolah and 'Eddie' Mabo to encourage and develop economic ventures among Torres Strait Islanders on the mainland and in the Torres Strait area. There were fourteen Meriam Directors with Mabo designated as Managing Director. The project had not got off the ground by the time Koiki died.

He emphasised the potential of the marine industry at Mer for trochus and crayfish and the employment that would be provided in an area where the chances of full employment were 'extremely remote'. Mabo envisaged thirty divers being employed and an average of 120 people being involved in the industry. It was an exciting prospect but needed capital and commitment which had not been found by the time of his death.[6]

At the same time, Koiki and Bonita were taking a small business course in Townsville with the intention of setting up a retail store on Murray Island to sell an array of goods, especially hardware and building materials which they knew were extremely expensive and generally unavailable.[7] Alternatively, they hoped they might be asked to run the existing store. The previous National Party Government had begun the process of transferring ownership of such economic enterprises to the indigenous residents of Aboriginal and Islander communities so this was not an unreasonable expectation, except for the fact that Mabo was involved in this immense challenge to the Queensland Government and was regarded with extreme hostility.

For a number of years Koiki had planned to return to live permanently at Mer and made at least eight visits, one almost a year long, between 1985 and 1991.[8] George Mye, long-time Chairman of Murray Island Council and currently, in 1996, Chairman of Darnley Island Council, told me that what made Koiki determined to fight for his land rights was the Queensland Government's decision that only residents of the Torres Strait Islands could have a say in Torres Strait Island affairs, including land ownership.[9] His claim for native title to inherit specific areas of Meriam land was a clear statement of intent to return.

The demands made upon Mabo's time by his legal counsel and the various court hearings waxed and waned over the ten years depending on the progress of the proceedings. Often, however, they resulted in stressful, frenetic activity. His involvement was possibly at its most intense during the 1989 Moynihan Inquiry into the facts of the High Court challenge. As Justice Moynihan noted in his determination:

> Eddie Mabo was an important witness in the plaintiff's case. He gave evidence on almost every aspect of the case and was examined, cross-examined and re-examined over 19 of the 66 days of sitting.[10]

Not only was he on the witness stand for such a prodigious amount of time, he also had to instruct his counsel, and find and interview witnesses to support his claim as the inquiry moved from Brisbane to Thursday Island to Murray Island and back to Brisbane. As well, he had to make special trips from Brisbane to Mackay and Townsville to gather more supporting witnesses. Although by no means complete, his diary from 2 May to 24 June 1989 reflects this constant round of activities associated with the case.

While the court was in session at Thursday Island, Koiki, Netta and their son Eddie took the opportunity one Sunday to visit St Paul's on Moa Island with three of his relatives. They inspected several projects including an experimental clay-brick house and a fishing project. Then they met up with some ex-Townsville Islanders who had moved back to the Torres Strait.

> All the families came together and we had small *kai kai* [feast] together at Oba's house. We slept at Gracie and Isobell Ware's house.
> The night was so perfect.[11]

The embracing warmth of Torres Strait Islander society contrasted sharply with the stress of the legal proceedings and the alien coldness of mainland culture: 'The night was so perfect.'

When not engaged in meetings, interaction with other Islanders, and liaising with his legal counsel, Koiki devoted himself to two activities derived from his Meriam culture: gardening and working on his boat. Koiki not only worked in his garden in suburban Townsville, he also planted Torres Strait Islander foods such as cassava and yams in the bush to grow wild.[12] They would then be collected for use in domestic cooking and for feasts. It was his boat, however, that took up his time while he was unemployed. It was a 21 foot (6.4 metre) bondwood Hartley with a 120-horsepower outboard motor that Koiki intended to take back to Mer to be used in the Meriam Trading Company. He and Netta envisaged growing vegetables on a commercial scale and using the boat to sell them on neighbouring islands. He had bought the boat second hand and had rebuilt much of it, creating a larger canopy with more seating beneath it. He was also fibreglassing it for use in the Torres Strait. It was a labour of great love. In July 1991, seven months before his death, he enrolled in a Coastal Navigation course at TAFE in preparation for the trip to Murray.[13] In 1996 the boat was standing at the side of his house, an ironic monument to the dreams of this energetic man.

The other permanent feature of his suburban home was an ancient, battered car parked perpetually on the footpath. The make changed occasionally but not the vintage. Koiki said to me, not long after we first met, that he realised when he first came to the mainland that he would need a car and that he would never be able to afford to have it regularly repaired and maintained commercially. 'So I said to myself, what man has made, I will have to learn to pull to pieces and put together again.' These may not have been his exact words, but this was the gist of his confident decision to master the intricacies of the motor car. I was impressed as I am one of the most mechanically inept people in Australia. Although Koiki did work on his vehicles that seemed extremely adventurous to me, his ambition obviously fell short of the achievement, as there was generally a car sitting in front of the Mabo home sadly in need of repairs. Sometimes he simply could not afford the parts.

Living on the dole for several years meant that money was always short. The man deemed one of the twenty 'most influential Australians in history' in the *Age* in 1995 was also his own housepainter and odd job man around the house.[14]

But beyond all of this there were the dreams of a life when he had won his court case and moved back permanently to Mer to his inheritance. All this was just an interlude before the final act of living back in the Torres Strait with his relatives and friends. Those Islanders who didn't support him or who contested his land claims were problems for the future that Koiki was confident he could attend to: they would see the rightness of his position.

In February 1991 Koiki Mabo returned to Mer for the last time to contest the Council elections. He organised a team of five under the name Meriam Tribal Council. He would contest the Chairman's position against the sitting incumbent, Ron Day. However, his nomination was rejected by the Returning Officer, Alo Tapim, because he had not met the local residency requirement of living continuously at Murray Island for the previous two years. Two people on Koiki's list were elected, Simeon Noah and Claude Mabo.[15]

Mabo prepared to challenge Tapim's decision and had an affidavit drawn up to present to the Queensland Supreme Court at Townsville. On legal advice, he decided not to proceed with the case as a stronger challenge from another Torres Strait Islander in another community against the rejection of his nomination had failed. This was the Rev. Nicey Sambo, Mabo's biological brother. Mabo's affidavit provides a fascinating insight into Koiki's perception of his past and his future. He was clearly positioning himself to become a political force in the Torres Strait. In the stillborn affidavit he asked to have the election to the Torres Strait Regional Council of ATSIC, due to be held one month after the local council elections, postponed to a later date so that he could be a candidate. His election as Chairman of Murray Island would have automatically made him a member of the Torres Strait Island Co-ordinating Council (IIC). These are very important bodies. Moreover, they would subsequently negotiate with the Commonwealth and Queensland Governments with regard to the increased autonomy for the Torres Strait promised for the year 2000.[16] This affidavit is interesting beyond its legal and political significance as it required Mabo to present his perspective of his relationship with Murray Island and the Meriam people:

1. I was born on Murray Island on the 26th day of June, 1936. I am currently a resident of Murray Island.

2. I left Murray Island at the age of 20 years of age and lived in Townsville until December 1988. From my departure until 1977 I was refused permission to return to Murray Island pursuant to legislation then in existence. From 1977 I began visiting two or three times per year until I eventually returned to Murray Island upon my children completing their education.

3. In late July 1990 my wife and myself went to Townsville to undertake a course of tuition in bookkeeping with James Concord. During this time I spent a month in Brisbane where I was a Guest Speaker at a law conference organised by the Aboriginal and Torres Strait Islander Research Foundation. I was invited to speak as I am one of the plaintiffs in the case of MABO AND OTHERS v THE STATE OF QUEENSLAND AND OTHERS which is presently before the High Court. My wife and I returned to Murray Island on 19th February, 1991 after completing the tutorial course.

4. Whilst I was in Townsville I resided with my children who reside at a house owned by my wife and myself at 23 Hibiscus Street, Cranbrook. It was at all times our intention to return to Murray Island upon completion of the course and [at] no time did we have any intentions of changing our permanent place of residence.

Alo Tapim's letter rejecting Mabo's nomination is quoted in the affidavit. Tapim referred to Election Manual rule 2(1) part 5 which stated that an intending candidate had to reside continuously in the area 'for not less than 24 months prior to the nomination day for an election for Island Council'. He continued:

It is noted that prior to the date of nomination you resided for at least a period of 6 months at 23 Hibiscus Street, Cranbrook, Townsville, Q. 4814. It is noted that you arrived at Murray Island on Tuesday 19th February, 1991 from your above residence. Your nomination is therefore disqualified in accordance with the above rule.[17]

Once again Queensland's legislation had become a source of dissent among Torres Strait Islanders. Mabo argued that he had at all times continuously 'maintained [his] residence at Murray Island' for the 24 months prior to 23 February 1991, the nomination date, except for his absence in Townsville doing a training course:

My sole period of absence was for the purposes of a training course at Townsville and I returned upon its completion ... There are no adult education facilities in the Torres Straits, and accordingly, it is necessary for residents to undertake such courses in Cairns and other large centres (such as Townsville).[18]

The rejection of Koiki Mabo's candidature remained unchallenged, Ron Day was re-elected chairman, and Koiki could not take up the leading role in the Torres Strait for which, he believed, his life's struggle had been preparing him.

Koiki Mabo's relationship with the Meriam people was often unsettling, even turbulent, and sometimes very stormy indeed. He contained within his person a threat to the established order and pattern of relationships as well as the promise of a very different, uncertain future, one which would fling off the authority of the white masters. He had fervent supporters and equally fervent opponents. On Murray Island he was often seen as the outsider, the man who had left under a cloud, and was absent for twenty years. On the mainland he had become possibly the best known Torres Strait Islander to black activists in the Aboriginal and Islander advancement movement, and to those in government circles and academia and to others sympathetic to black advancement. In the Torres Strait he was seen by some as an intruder, and an anti-government radical critical of those who had authority within government structures or who were willing to work along with government policies. Moreover, his return would challenge anyone occupying land that Mabo believed he had inherited. In Melanesia one of the commonest causes of community friction derives from disputes over land ownership. This is certainly exemplified on Murray Island, where the Queensland Government kept records of law cases which they allowed to be decided by Islander customary law. One of Mabo's lawyers, Greg McIntyre, described the Meriam as one of the most litigious people in the world.[19] Mabo's activism was also encompassed within a personality that expected to be listened to with respect. After all, he had made himself an authority on Torres Strait Islander culture who could educate and guide white lawyers and academics as no one had ever done before.

Although his diaries and other personal papers are by no means complete, they contain ample evidence of the tensions and conflicts that were part and parcel of Mabo's public life. Even the still-born Meriam Trading Company scheme was a cause of dissension, as his diary entries indicate:

While at Sebeg I saw Mr Dipoma's goods inside the house built by Kebisu Fred on my land at Sebeg.

On my return to Deo I met Mr Kalia Noah on the road in front of Kabere's Jarb[?]. I asked him who was taking care of Dipoma's belongings. He told me he was; I then asked him if it was possible to move Dipoma's things out of the house so I can prepare the land for the freezer to be built.

He said there will have to be a court case over it between Dipoma and myself. As late Kebisu Fred had willed Sebeg to Dipoma and that Dipoma had appointed Kalia Noah to take care of the village under the Meriam Traditional Law.

I told Noah that the land at Sebeg and all adjoining territories of Gardening land above Sebeg was never owned by Naina Fred as my father was the rightful owner of Sebeg. It was through my father's (Benny Mabo) orders after the war that Naina Fred began occupying Sebeg when we moved to Las.

Kalia also mentioned that he had heard Goi my great Grandmother only owned Eum, a gardening land above Sebeg. According to my father and Celuia, Goi owned all the land including Sebeg, Sebeg Mager, Baugered, Waber, Eum, Ai, Mikia-Nunur, Arpet and Dion.[20]

The Meriam Enterprises Scheme had even more dramatic consequences, as Koiki noted in his diary on 7 January 1988:

Sat at Figtree Shade with Wilfred Tapau. Frank Ansey came over to us and started to pick fight with me. The reason for his argument was that he did object to Meriam Enterprises establishing a freezer here at Mer. I tried to talk some sense into him but he could not listen. So he started to punch me. First he drove a punch right cross aimed at my left jaw but instead landed on my left shoulder. I felt I could not get out of this one except to stand up and let him have it. I landed a left hook on his jaw and he fell to the ground for the first time. He stood up and wanted another so I landed another, this time a straight right, and big Frank went down on his knees, he got up and still wanted another, I was gasping for breath by then, but nevertheless I wanted to make him sleep, so this time he copped a straight right to the left side of the jaw and he went down and went to kiss the dirt for a much longer period. Until Denis Passi came around and helped him up to his feet. I was by that time really 'had it'. Went to the shop and Lela Noah gave me a can of Fanta. After an hour I walked back to Deo.

On another occasion two Islanders wanted to fight Koiki on election night in 1991. He dismissed this challenge with contempt:

> After counting the votes Alo T and I walked out of Council office and met Trugga and Pomoi Salee, who were drunk and offered to fight me because I was an opposition to the Council. I walked away telling them that I do not discuss local politics with drunken bums.[21]

When he believed a fellow Islander had assisted the Queensland Government's case against the Murray Island traditional land claim, he was moved to an impassioned eloquence:

> As a first named plaintiff with a long track record of involvement in the struggles against white oppression, I am extremely disturbed that your Mr Meriam Man (a Murray Islander) ... accompanied Mr Polsard when he visited such people as Mr Eses Gesah, Ms Merinda Mabo and Mr George Kudub and prompted leading questions in order to allow the state solicitor to detect possible loopholes for attack in our claims for traditional ownership of plots of lands in question.
>
> I am equally disturbed and so are other plaintiffs and witnesses to think that [an] organisation such as yours which was born as a result of similar struggle against the state oppression, had to harbour a collaborator and a pimp for the oppressor of our fellow Black People ...

I would presume that you, like the rest of us, do make positive stance as to which side of the fence you're at. If such is your case also, one only finds one self in a difficult position of divorcing one set of Aboriginal struggle from another, may they be Land Rights, Education, Housing, Health, Child Welfare, Legal or Cultural, to my politically dominated thinkings they all fall into one heading — 'The Aboriginal Struggle', regardless of individuals involved. On the other hand, I totally fail to understand the motives behind those who occupy paid positions and quite shamelessly regard themselves as being involved in the struggle by working for Aboriginal and Islander interests and betterment. [This] is a mere farce in anyone's language, particularly when one finds the so-called involved people [allowing] themselves to be used by our oppressors who are endeavouring destruction of Aboriginal and Islander land rights.[22]

It is not certain that Mabo sent this letter. He may simply have been letting off steam.

In 1995 Netta Mabo reflected bitterly on the stress Koiki and the family lived under as a result of his involvement with black organisations in Townsville and the opposition he encountered on Murray. She stated that, when he worked for a black housing cooperative, he attempted to get tenants to pay back rents they owed and had to evict some people. Continued government funding, she said, depended on a more businesslike approach.

… it stirred up a lot of ill-will, and he got a lot of death threats. Koiki would come home from meetings and cry about the lack of support, and we were afraid at night. We had all those children in the house.

Netta Mabo also reflected on the opposition he had encountered at Murray Island:

When Koiki went home to Murray Island, they told him they didn't want his 'ideas from the south'. They put him out of meetings, offered to take him outside to fight, and called the police to remove him: the same people who gained so much from his work.

After he died, I went there and they let me know that my 30-odd year marriage to Koiki didn't make me a local, an Islander … Our eldest son, Eddie, is in charge of the whole lot there now, all our family things. They can't say the same about Eddie, that he's not an Islander. He has his father's blood in his veins.[23]

The people who opposed Koiki Mabo will, of course, have different perspectives. Here, however, I am presenting his perspective of his life. Netta Mabo's reflections support this picture of a very active activist who saw himself pitted against the white political structure, but often with opposition from the people he was trying to lead. Members of an ethnic group generally find their warmest, most meaningful relationships within it; sometimes it is also the source of the most intense animosities.

Koiki Mabo never buckled under opposition from within the black community, although at times he was clearly hurt by it. He took positions and argued from them with a great deal of self-confidence, as his diaries indicate. And he always had his supporters. Moreover, while participating enthusiastically in Islander society on the mainland and in the Torres Strait, he was often critical of it. Indirectly this often manifested itself at meetings as he tried to drive through his point of view.

Essentially he had both insider and outsider perspectives of his own culture. This is revealed in a number of incidents recounted in his diary. On Murray Island in 1988 he was very critical of the medical attention being given to a very sick Islander:

> The medical staff attended him and gave him oxygen every four hours.
> To me that was not good enough as I recall being put on oxygen as soon as I entered the Hospital with a chest complaint.
> I got quite annoyed with the Council for being complacent and also reluctant about implementing better services.[24]

No doubt the Islander Council were annoyed also at the criticism. Ironically, as Koiki noted in his diary, the patient had improved by the next day.[25]

An undated discussion paper he prepared for the Netat Urapun Buai Progressive Association indicated clearly his critique of the colonialist situation the Islanders had experienced and his criticism of previous Meriam inaction:

> The history of our road on Murry Is dates back to the time of Mamoos. Who were placed in power by the Queensland Colonial Government. The Mamoos was to represent Queen Victoria of England. So therefore our roads were established over 110 years ago. Scores of councillor have came and went but none was able to improve our roads beyond the third world standards. Even in this rich Australian environment, this part of the rich and lucky country continues to be the third world sector of this rich nation. Why is it we may ask that such labels are only applicable to Black communities throughout Australian states.[26]

The Queensland Supreme Court sat at Murray Island in May 1989 with Judge Moynihan presiding. Koiki returned with Netta and his eldest son, Eddie, and was shocked at the untidy state of the community. He was worried that this could create a bad impression on the judge. Moreover, Yarra Bank Films were preparing to shoot *Land Bilong Islanders*:

> Upon arrival I was very disgusted with what I saw, piles and piles of rubbish. It seems as though every Torres Strait Islander used Mer as a rubbish dump. The place was lousy with rotten smell from bags and bags of rubbish. Somebody has to clean the place up before the judge arrives here on Monday. George Kudub, Thomas Mabo and Nanai Sailor agreed to help Eddie jnr and I to clean up the place.[27]

Saturday, 20 May, was a day of varied activity:

> At Mer. Clean up day. Carted rubbish which was piled up in front of every house for months. Started cleaning at Umar Reserve and worked towards Bearer. Each house required at least 2 large trailer loads of garbage. New dump established ...
> Also did some filming with Yarra Bank Films Ltd.
> And I also interviewed witnesses in between carting rubbish.[28]

They did not finish carting rubbish until 3.30 pm on Sunday, 21 May:

> At least the place looks reasonably clean with no smelly garbage bags laden with maggots and flies can no longer be seen on the side of the roads.
>
> No Sunday Service for us.[29]

Koiki had obviously been a thorn in the side of conservative Islanders for a long time, especially Islander councillors. As late as January 1988, he was informed that he was not welcome at a conference sponsored by the Torres Strait Island Co-ordinating Council (ICC) which was attended by 400 people. In his diary Koiki noted that Steve Mam, one of Queensland's leading Torres Strait Islander activists, had been forced to tell the ICC that unless Mabo was invited he, Steve Mam, would not attend. Koiki's fares were paid and he delivered three papers: 1. How the Name Magani Malu Kes came into existence, 2. The Proposed New Aboriginal and Torres Strait Commission, and 3. An Alternative to Sovereign Independence. The call for 'sovereign independence' was accepted as 'official policy' of the conference. An Independence Working Party was elected with Koiki as a member.[30]

Koiki's response to Christianity varied over time, but he was seen by many Islanders as a non-Christian. His greatest objection, however, was to its association with colonialist oppression, a perspective that was probably not appreciated by the strongly Christian Islander community. His diary entry for 1 July 1985, the day on which Islanders of every denomination celebrate The Coming of the Light, indicates this clearly. This ceremony commemorates the arrival of the first missionaries in the Torres Strait on 1 July 1871 and is for many the most important day of the Christian year. They have made Christianity, the faith of the colonisers, their religion and given it Torres Strait Islander

forms, in association with a number of established denominations. Some of their congregations in North Queensland have a
totally Islander membership. But in Townsville in 1985, in an
historic re-enactment, an almost desperate attempt was made to
dramatise how the light of Christianity had shone into the night
of traditional paganism.

> Left the office and went to Saint Stephen's Church, Railway Estate.
> At 12.00 noon there was a church service and I went in and took
> part in the mass. The Bishop of North Qld, John Lewis, conducted
> the mass.
>
> After the service at approximately 3 pm there was an enactment
> of the 'Coming of the Light' in which several people painted
> themselves with charcoal or black paint. What a disgrace and an
> insult of their own people.
>
> Little that we realise that celebration of such occasions are only
> a praise of white supremacy, plunder, rape and land robbery by the
> white settlers.
>
> I am beginning to worry just how long before we are able to free
> ourselves from the Christian mentality and fear of Christ, to be our
> whole selves again.
>
> Through these type of activities we are viewed as stupid and
> careless and abusive in the light of our own people and culture.[31]

The Reverend David Passi, in *Land Bilong Islanders*, elo-
quently argued that the traditional Meriam religion was fulfilled
by the Christian faith but that God had not been absent from
Meriam society prior to the coming of Europeans. The traditional
religion had an integral relationship with Christianity, in much
the same way as the theology of the Old Testament had with that
of the New Testament.

There was no hint of this in the drama that unfolded that day.
Mabo found it a humiliating experience. Melanesian people are
among the darkest people on the planet. Making some blacker
so that others could play the white missionary roles seemed
absurd. He was proud to be black.

The Mabo Papers reveal a more complex, spiritual dimension to the political activist in these last years. In a short speech of welcome delivered to the first National Torres Strait Islander Conference in Brisbane, 22–25 June 1991, Mabo clearly referred to God in typically Christian terms that his large Islander audience could relate to:

> Welcome to all my friends and delegates and a very good morning to all of you. Welcome to all leaders and spokespeople and employees. Most of us have travelled long distances. I welcome and appreciate your determination to be here at this conference. Despite the fact that you may have had very important tasks to do back home with your organisations ... I also thank Our Heavenly Father for assisting Iina in their endeavours to get us together at this most critical time. And most of all many thanks to Iina Board of Directors and the staff who made it possible for us to come together today as one people.
>
> I would also like to express my sympathy to those ... who had left us and departed to new life beyond. I wish that sweet memories of their association with us will remain with us for ever. For those of us remaining must strive to achieve the utmost for our people, while sharing love and continued friendship with our people.[32]

The speech, made seven months before his death, has the ring of confidence of one who is an accepted leader of his people and feels at one with them. He had refused to attend unless his wife's fare to the conference was met. It was.[33]

On 15 March 1988 at what Koiki vainly hoped would be the final hearing of *Mabo and Others, Mer Island's Traditional Land Claims* before the Full Bench of the High Court in Canberra, he made a moving entry. It expressed the tension and spiritual dimension of the occasion:

> The writ for this case was issued in 1981 by the plaintiff. All of the hearing has been won by us. I hope My *Agud* will still be with me on these final days of our Land Claims: I know *Agud* will be with me.[34]

In the privacy of his diary his expression of faith reached back past the Christianity of colonialism to the source of spiritual power revealed to his ancestors.

To the outside world Koiki Mabo was the quintessential political activist. He spoke to small and large groups, black and white, about Aboriginal and Islander advancement and of the essential place of the Meriam Traditional Land Claim to this movement. He also prepared a series of notices or handouts to increase the support begun at the 1981 Conference held at James Cook University when the Islanders decided to take their High Court action.[35] Mabo utilised press commentary on the legal process to present the Islander case and his own unique political perspective. He used an article in the *Sydney Morning Herald* on 30 April 1985, 'Islanders take white Australia to the High Court', to create a very effective one-page notice introducing himself to a wider audience and attacking the Queensland Government for its opposition to the Meriam claim to Native Title. He explained and rejected the Coast Islands Declaratory Act which the Queensland Government passed in 1985 especially to defeat the Meriam High Court challenge. Mabo pointed to the racist motivation of this law. The journalist referred to it as 'apparently unprecedented'. Mabo also attacked the Queensland Government's Deeds of Grant in Trust Legislation, passed in 1984 to acknowledge for the first time in Queensland's history that Aboriginal and Torres Strait Islander people had some sort of title to their land. This was the National Party's attempt to placate the Aboriginal Advancement Movement which had threatened to destroy Queensland's international reputation at the 1982 Brisbane Commonwealth Games. The Deeds of Grant in Trust were given to Queensland's Aboriginal and Torres Strait Islander communities by 1987. Only Murray Island refused to accept the Trust Deeds because of the pending High Court challenge and the uncertainty about how the Queensland offer would affect the Islanders' claim.

The *Herald* article quoted Mabo:

> The Government has long used Islanders to boost the economy of this State. This included cheap labour they took from my father.
>
> Now they are trying to stop us having land we are entitled to ... My family has occupied the land for hundreds of years before Captain Cook was born. They are now trying to say I cannot own it.[36]

Some elements of the national media had sensed the ramifications of the struggle that had been joined. A splendid photograph of Mabo accompanied the article while a map showed readers where Murray Island is situated. Above and below the article was Mabo's address to Torres Strait Islander people:

> Hi,
>
> My name is Edward Mabo, my island name is <u>Koiki</u>. I was born at Mer (Murray Island). I now live in Townsville. I will be returning soon to my home island to live.
>
> In this paper cutting, you will read about the test case I am heading on our behalf in the High Court of Australia.
>
> If this case comes in our favour, this would mean we will not be paying rent to the DNA anymore. As our islands will become recognised by Queensland Government as our own private land.
>
> On the 9th April 1985 Queensland Government made a new law which will enable Aboriginal and Island people to lease traditional lands. They also passed another law which says that after we became part of Queensland in 1879, we lost our rights to our land and no compensation will be claimed by us. We admit that we became part of Queensland in 1879 but our land rights exist and we want our rights to be fully recognised by the Queensland Government. Because we believe these laws are made by men and can be undone by men.
>
> Present Queensland Government is a friendly enemy of the black people as they like to give you the Bible and take away your land.

We should stop calling them Boss and we should not give them our respect.[37]

The Islanders' lawyers described the Coast Islands Declaratory Act as 'a bombshell'. The Mabo Papers contain another notice prepared by Koiki in Miriam and English. An undated article from the *Sydney Morning Herald*, 'Qld acts to head off High Court', is the centrepiece of this handout, with an appeal in Miriam on the left and one in English on the right. This time 'Qld Govt is our Friendly Enemy' is used as Mabo's heading. The article itself goes into more detail about the purpose of the Queensland Coast Islands Declaratory Bill 1985. The Deputy Premier, Mr Bill Gunn, made it emphatically clear that the purpose of the legislation was to confirm the 1879 annexation, to specifically rule out retrospectively any native title that might have existed, and to deny the Island residents any claim for compensation: in short to circumvent the proceedings before the High Court. It was claimed once again that it was unprecedented for a government to legislate to nullify High Court decision making. The article also clearly relates the nature of the Meriam native title claim to the High Court. Mabo consequently utilised the *Herald* article to communicate the nature of the claim and the opposition. Then in Meriam Mir and in English he urged the Islanders to cease cooperating with the Queensland Government in any way that could harm the land claim or indicate an acceptance of its sovereignty on Murray Island. He even urged the return to a pre-colonial lifestyle to throw off Queensland Government control:

Qld Govt is our Friendly Enemy

There are several things we must do to make our land claim to be stronger and these are as follows:

1. We must restrict our contacts with the Department of Community Services.

2. We must restrict acceptance of services offered by DCS.

3. We must refuse to co-operate with State Govt. officers when they are on visit to our home islands.

4. We must instruct our councillors not to order any more DNA houses to be built on our islands.

5. We must refuse to pay rent for our existing houses, that has already been built on our traditional lands unless sale agreements with the DCS making sure that no lease agreements are signed, which will undermine our traditional land ownership.

6. We must be proud to live in our own palm leaf houses like our fathers before us. By doing this we will pay no rent to DNA.[38]

A third one-page notice he prepared at the time used an undated cutting from an unnamed newspaper entitled, ' "Historic benchmark" for Aborigines, Islanders'. This seems more like a press release from the Queensland Minister for Aboriginal and Islander Affairs, Bob Katter Jr, explaining the concept of black capitalism he was developing in association with his 1985 Deeds of Grant in Trust legislation. Within the trust land, Aboriginal or Torres Strait Islander residents could apply for perpetual leases of land for homes, businesses or farms. Blocks of land could also be sold or mortgaged to other indigenous residents to promote economic growth and self-sufficiency. The white dream of self-sufficiency for Aboriginal reserves and missions dates back to the nineteenth century. To it this time had been grafted the dynamic of free-enterprise capitalism. The cooperativeness articulated through kinship inherent in Aboriginal and Torres Strait Islander societies was to be replaced by an acquisitive individualism in which a prosperous class of entrepreneurs would emerge to offer employment to those less motivated or less able.

Mabo thundered at the Islanders like an Old Testament prophet in Meriam Mir and English insisting that no Torres Strait

Island Council should lease land under this whiteman's legislation. The land was not the white government's to dispose of.

FOR YOUR INFORMATION
THIS IS VERY IMPORTANT WE MUST UNDERSTAND IT
Able mir ge osmelu Townsville nus pepa ge. Able gerger ge April 12, 1985.

E detautli kega. Gair agei a pako gair Kaur Buaigize tabara ge lisem waikerare. State Govman lam.

Agei a Kaur buai ra Minister Bob Katter de able gelar dispili E datautli, kega Queensland era more debe gelar deke kemer-kemer Australia.

But kari Lawyer gize e natagerda kega Queensland era able kerkar gelar pe.
NOLE ABKOREP MERBIM TORRES STRAIT LEGIZEM IKE. ABLEGLAM MERIBA GEDPE AU ZOGO-ZOGO GED A AU GELAR-GELAR GED NARID, MERBI ARER KER KER LAM.
Meriba Arer ge urder taba gedge keuba kole bakarki Australiage. Therefore gair Torres Strait legize nole Tabara ged ko lisem waikerare.

Torres Strait Council should not permit any Islander to lease any part of these Islands.
WE MUST INSIST AND DEMAND THAT QUEENSLAND GOVERNMENT RECOGNIZE OUR TRADITIONAL NATIVE TITLE TO THESE ISLANDS.
We must not make any attempt to lease our own ancestral land as we have full rights to these lands inherited through our Fathers before us.
THE PUBLIC MUST ALSO KEEP AN EYE ON THE ACTIONS OF THE COUNCIL. IF THEY MAKE ANY MOVE IN FAVOUR OF THE NEW LAND LAW, THE PUBLIC SHOULD DISMISS THE WHOLE COUNCIL, AS THESE ACTIONS ARE AGAINST OUR OWN INTERESTS.

                                        E. MABO   16.4.85[39]

The three notices reveal clearly the David and Goliath nature of the struggle that had been joined. With the slogan 'Qld Govt is our Friendly Enemy', Mabo encapsulated the previous half-century of soft control which had resulted in a grateful dependence. In order to achieve equality and their land, the Islanders had to break the colonialist chains that bound them.

Throughout his life, and certainly in the last seven years of his life, Mabo maintained contact with Murray Island not only by the frequent visits he made after 1977 but also through letters, by telephone and through discussion with Townsville's Islander community. He also met visitors from other mainland communities, such as Steve Mam from Brisbane, or from the Torres Strait. People from Murray Island contacted him, or he them, for a variety of reasons, some because of local political developments which impinged upon land rights. The entry of 4 November 1991 reads:

> Phoned Henry Kabere at Murray Island. He told me that the Councillors from Mer had gone to Darwin to experience the Ab land right laws in NT. I advised him to tell everyone to wait for our court Mabo and Oths v Qld decision.[40]

On 28 November Koiki was unable to stand up because of the cancer in his spine and was only able to speak in a hoarse whisper. On the previous day Goby Noah and his wife Mary had called to see him and George Kudub had rung from Mer to inquire about his health. On 28 November the entry reads:

> Noretta and Pana Jack Wailu phoned but could hardly speak to them because of my voice. Pana said about the public meeting at Mer about the Land Rights legislation in NT and Council want to accept the same on Mer.
>
> Phoned the Council but Pana Jack Wailu had left the phone. Instead Ms Elsie Kabere answered and I gave her our house phone no. for her Dad Henry.[41]

Koiki Mabo died two months later on 21 January 1992. The Murray Island Council did not apply for their Deed of Grant in Trust. They waited for the High Court Decision which, on 3 June

1992, recognised that native title had existed from time immemorial not only for the Meriam people of Murray Island but for all Aboriginal and Torres Strait Islander people. With specific reference to the Murray Islands, the High Court order declared that:

> ... the Meriam people are entitled as against the whole world to possession, occupation, use and enjoyment of the lands of the Murray Islands.[42]

Koiki Mabo's diary for 1992 contains only seven entries. Some are concerned with the recognition of traditional land inheritance in Australia, particularly that which he inherited from his father, Benny Mabo, and which he expected his family to inherit after his death. He realised this was clearly imminent. Some are about his family, his concern for their health and his worry about the effects of 'foreign matters' such as tobacco and alcohol. He also stipulated clearly how his property should be distributed and how his wife, Netta, should be respected. The fragments presented here of Koiki Mabo's life are part of the love story between Koiki, Mer and the Meriam people which expands and embraces broader social and political issues. At the personal level it is the love story of Bonita and Koiki Mabo. Like all love stories both of these have had their stormy passages. And, as with so many love stories, death intervened to leave them unfinished.

For Koiki and Bonita Mabo, however, the tragedy of death was followed by the triumph of the High Court decision which restored to Aboriginal and Torres Strait Islander people the recognition of their native title to their land. They could now negotiate from a much stronger position with the colonial governments that dispossessed them and the multinational companies that wished to exploit land deemed still to possess native title. The struggle of Koiki and Bonita Mabo and those who supported them had helped to open a new chapter in Australia's history.

It is fitting to conclude with Koiki Mabo's own words written in the last weeks of his life. Facing a soon and certain death, he re-stated his traditional claims to land which had been rejected by Justice Moynihan and in so doing rejected Moynihan's conclusions. The handwriting is shaky, even spidery, at the beginning of this entry as he was presumably writing it lying down. As he proceeded, it became stronger and clearer. I have had to guess a number of the words.

> On previously known Mabo Land in HCA [High Court of Australia] is to be known as 'Koit Land' which starts from Las 14A and Dam to 'Miear' near the Air Strip because Koit died with one of his wives 'Anpi' long before his boys reached the age of manhood. All his land was never divided to his sons but instead his sons selected their own sites to garden.
>
> Modee or Modi or Misi — the oldest of Koit's sons — married 'Jeub' who came from a line of Jib Family also known as Kagaroo Family. Modee after marrying his wife Jeub went to live on her land and gardened on her lands as well. He only occupied Korkor near Wenoe(?) Korkor and down to 'Tar'.
>
> Koit's other son Oroto or Oth was adopted to Dowar by the first Mamoos of Dowar, so his rights were surrendered by Koit. He therefore has no claim on Koit's land. Oroto or his descendants have no claims on Koit's land.
>
> Koit's other son Mabo remained in possession of all Koit's land. He lived at Las. At some time he moved to Leiwag and Ulag then to Ibir below 'Semar' and then at 'Sebeg'. Mabo had most use of all the land of his father, Koit, his wife's land from her father's side & also from her Mother Goi's land from Sebeg, to all other land in Komet area, including — Sebeg Mager, Beaugred, Man-vi Taboeb in front of Tarau Gray's 'Taboeb', Eum, Arpet, now being used by Henry Kabere, Al and Duri. Mabo also had sole use of his Mother's land as well including Ulag, Crlng Mager, Kebi Saurem, Wabodmop

and Tarbid. Mabo and his wife Akazi also had sole use of 'Gasu land' including Leiwag, and Werir Kes, land above the plateau [?] is SAUREM which goes past the road into the rain forest to the bamboo patch way up into Kirr where there are heaps and heaps of rocks together representing Kapmariri Stone of the Te-pi-pi and Te Saber-Saber or through the story of Meb and Irwami Deo.

I learned all these stories from my father Benny Mabo and his wife Maiga Mabo and I also experienced how the land was used during my upbringing.

E. Mabo
4.1.92[43]

An entry on 2 January spelt out how he wanted his Townsville property disposed of if Netta Mabo decided to sell her half-share in their home.

The final decision will be hers and hers alone ... The doctor was not so sure whether the trip to Brisbane Radium Institute was going to make me better or make me worse. But whatever may happen to me I want all of you to take good care of your Mum, don't abuse her in any way. Let her be the central figure in your lives just like both of us have been in your lives.[44]

An entry made in the last week of his life while he was in hospital in Brisbane again expressed the centrality in his thoughts of his wife, his family and his land at Mer. However, he was still looking towards the future of the island of his birth where he, himself, wished to be buried.

After 2 pm I went out with Edward, Gwen and Netta to New Farm Park for the afternoon. Brenda and Nathan met us there and we stayed out until 8 pm before they brought me back to the hospital.

I spoke to Mr Edward B Mabo my son about the possibility of his mother returning to Las village at Mer. Bonita E Mabo is to be treated as a queen of Las at all times ...

As for the land at Sebeg currently occupied by Marwer Dipoma or his adopted son. Must be claimed as Goi Land for inclusion on Mabo's Holdings — it seems that this land of Sebeg was let by

Matherena Fred, late wife of Kebisu Fred, to look after their things at the house at Sebeg while Mrs M Fred came to Townsville in app. 1964–67. This was supposed to be a short leave of absence by Matherina Fred from Mer but this they continued until both Kebisu Fred and his wife Matherina Fred had died in Townsville — without leaving anything about the land transaction of Sebeg in writing anywhere.

This practice is not common in Meriam traditional laws in terms of caretakership. In most cases the caretakership never lasted after one of the parties had died and the said land or lands in question returned to new 'Ged Kem le' [landowner] of the true blood line under traditional lineage or placed under proper blood line for claims.[45]

His ten years' experience in Australian law is clearly evident in the last paragraph as is his lifetime's learning of Meriam custom.

Another entry in these last weeks brings together very movingly Koiki's love for his wife, his long commitment to his struggle for justice and the recognition of native title to land.

Netta, Selena, Maria came to see me at Ward 4AB TGH [Townsville General Hospital]. They stayed until 10 pm. After they had left me the rest of the night was not so bad. I lay in bed thinking about the future and how I would like it to be even if I am not there.

I thought about the struggles I have been through over the past years since 1963 to 1991 or to the beginning of 1992, while the rest of Black Australia awaits with me for the High Court decision to be brought down at any time. Or would it be in time for me to receive it and make further decisions on the outcome of that decision — for further actions if this decision is not favourable?

If I am not around I want my children to work closely with my lawyers and other advisors to plan future actions. Working closely with other plaintiffs is also important.

I also thought about how my wife, the most important person in my life, has stuck to me over many hardships and hurdles in life but somehow we made it, perhaps better than others. To me my wife has been the most adorable person, a friend closest in my life, a most wonderful lover, and we loved every minute of our lives together.

Over the years we were stuck together like a Gep [sucker fish] to Baizam [shark]. She allowed Baizam to make first move in making decisions affecting our Daily Lives. Decisions re run of the house and children were decisions for Mother. I was also classed as her baby, and she could push me around at Home any which way — I just loved it, every bit of it.[47]

9

Return to Mer

On Mer they welcomed home 'the great man'. The title had been used by the Reverend Dave Passi and others who spoke on the day of his tombstone unveiling in Townsville, and it was now used in speeches as the burial and tombstone unveiling was repeated on Mer. For twenty years prior to 1977 Koiki Mabo had been prevented from returning to Mer by one pretext or another but now the Council of Elders received him with the greatest dignity and respect. After the desecration of Mabo's grave Bonita Mabo and the children immediately, and with emphatic certainty, declared that his body and the imposing tombstone would be taken home to Mer where he had always wanted to be buried. The desecration ensured he would return home for good.

The elders on Mer agreed emphatically, with their customary dignity, that they wanted him buried at Mer where they could respect and care for him. Much of the irritation, suspicion, and bitterness of the past had actually begun to die with Koiki on 21 January 1992. The Murray Islanders had come to his funeral in Townsville in great numbers to pay their respects to the man, and to the great battle he had fought for their rights to their land for so many years. The High Court decision on 3 June 1992 had confirmed his greatness not only in their eyes but in the eyes of so many other Australians who were stunned at the achievements of the five plaintiffs: Edward Koiki Mabo, Dave Passi, James Rice and the two other plaintiffs who had died earlier in the proceedings, Celuia Mapo Salee and Sam Passi. Now he would be buried in his land at Las, the burial ground of the ancient spiritual leaders, *zogo le*, of the Malo-Bomai cult that had dominated Meriam life, given them the law and unified the eight often fractious clans of Mer. This was signified by the octopus, whose form Malo had taken on his epic journey before he arrived at Las. Each of the eight tentacles of the octopus represented a clan, and the strong central body was the unity they had achieved through Malo and his teachings: *Malo Ra Gelar*, Malo's Law. Malo's power encompassed both *agud*.

The Malo dance, performed for the first time for eighty years at his tombstone unveiling on Mer, confirmed for many at Las Mabo's position as a spiritual leader in the ancient line of ancestors, *zogo le*, of the awe-inspiring *agud*, Malo-Bomai. Many Meriam now saw this dual deity as the forerunner of Christ. Christianity had been brought by the missionaries in 1871 but the Islanders had known God's presence 'from time imme-morial'. The *zogo le* had officiated at the sacred ritual, worn the sacred masks, and had Malo's sacred power to guide the Meriam. Mabo would be buried at Las, where bones of some of his ancestors could be seen, revealed to Meriam view by Mer's wind and rain. Some at Las even used the term *Ait*, the one Justice Moynihan had claimed was not a title but a personal name on which Mabo had no claim. But Justice Moynihan was now an irrelevance. The Meriam would make their own decisions and reach their own conclusions.

After Mabo's funeral on 1 February 1992, his family decided to have his tombstone unveiling on 3 June 1995, a Saturday, as this would coincide with the Queen's Birthday weekend and would allow people time to travel to and from the Torres Strait and other distant places. It would also coincide with the Mabo Day Celebrations which had been organised annually since 1993 by the Council of Elders to commemorate the High Court decision brought down on 3 June 1992. There had been an earlier celebration in 1992, organised to coincide with Bryan Keon-Cohen's visit to Townsville to explain the High Court decision soon after it had been delivered. In 1993 and 1994 there had been public celebrations in Townsville's Mall on 3 June, followed by Islander feasts and dancing at night. Clearly this was going to be an annual event. The publicity given to the decision, the enthusiasm of much of the media, and the wide support received from the Australian people had convinced Islander leaders that this was a commemoration for all Australians. It had seemed an important step in the reconciliation process which the Islanders could celebrate with the rest of the Townsville community. While the significance of the High Court decision was still being endlessly debated and the battle to create acceptable native title legislation had been furious, no one expected the vicious obscenity of the tombstone desecration.

In Koiki's words on an earlier occasion, the day had been 'so perfect'. The march through Townsville's main street had been punctuated by Meriam dances at the end of each block. There had been many speeches of tribute in the City Mall from prominent black and white Australians, and the swooping, soaring Islander voices captivated the crowd with their hymns and the Torres Strait and Murray Island anthems.

The tombstone unveiling had been moving and dignified, yet also an intimate occasion for family and friends. Mrs Annita Keating was present, representing the Prime Minister, as well as Robert Tickner, the Federal Minister for Aboriginal Affairs. That night, the feast following the tombstone unveiling had been held in one of the largest halls in Townsville.

The crowds at the City Mall and the tombstone unveiling had received an open invitation to attend the feast that night, and as they entered the hall they were confronted by a huge model of an octopus, woven from coconut leaves, with its eight tentacles stretched out on long tables that held the food for the feast. Each table was dedicated to one of the Meriam clans; and the great *agud*, Malo, presided at the Christian feast. A haunting, dirge-like lament of pre-Christian origin accompanied the stately Malo dances which the dancers from Mer had been preparing for months. The evening was a joyous affirmation of life, the end of the grieving period, 'the end of sorry', yet, of all the dances performed that night it was this mournful lament that had the most impact. It did not seem like a premonition of things to come; it just seemed appropriate to have this ancient echo from the Meriam past present in suburban Townsville to celebrate Mabo's tombstone unveiling. The events throughout the whole day had seemed to reach out to all Australians. It had all seemed 'so perfect'.

The next morning one of Mabo's close friends, Ted Wymara, returned to the cemetery to farewell his friend before returning home to Cairns and found that the grave had been desecrated. Eight swastikas had been sprayed in red paint from a pressure can on the black marble tombstone and the word 'Abo' sprayed twice. Red paint had also been sprayed elsewhere around the grave to disfigure it. The bronze image of Mabo's smiling face, which had been fixed into the marble with long bolts, had been removed without the bolts being cut or the marble being damaged. Someone had apparently been in the crowd, or visited the grave after the crowd left in the afternoon, and returned with a can of paint and a tool that allowed the bolts attached to the bust to be drawn or levered out of the marble. The racists responsible have still not been found, nor has the bronze face of Mabo been recovered.

Mabo's family and friends were devastated by this demonstration of obscene hatred, as were people throughout Australia. Most of Townsville's white community were shocked that this could happen in their city. Many felt a sense of deep shame, and a 'Community Rally for Respect and Understanding' was organised for the following Saturday, just one week after the tombstone unveiling. The sense of shock, dismay and disgust was shared widely throughout Australia and was reflected in the extensive media coverage. Prime Minister Keating offered financial support for the family's decision to return Mabo's remains and the tombstone to Mer and, as a result, the Australian Air Force made six Caribou flights to ferry Mabo relatives to Mer while commercial and charter flights brought other mourners. In her grief and shock, Bonita Mabo had earlier exclaimed that she would sell her house if necessary to meet the costs involved.

Koiki had asked Donald Whaleboat to make sure nothing happened to his house in Hibiscus Street after he died.[1]

> He wanted it to be preserved at all times because it was there that everything started: his dreams, his visions, the inspiration that resulted in his crusade to help his people and to seek justice, his involvement in black organisations, the Black Community School,

the university and finally the *Mabo* case. He wanted this house to be a museum of his life's work and an inspiration to others.

The decision to move Mabo's remains to Mer, even if it meant selling his house, reflects the hurt, the disgust and the despair of his family.

The September school holidays were chosen as the most suitable time for this unique event. The Meriam elders made a narrow, winding path from the small aerodrome to Las on the opposite side of the island from the main village which had grown up around the old mission site. The procession halted twice before reaching Las and the coffin was placed on a bier, *takar*, covered with a woven palm-leaf mat, where an elder quoted the words of Malo:

> Meriam … when you walk through the path nobody will take notice where you are going in and how you are coming out.[2]

The procession then moved on to Las where Mabo's body lay in state for three days, from Friday until the funeral ceremony the following Monday. The mourners sat into the first evening with Bonita Mabo around the coffin of polished wood with its gleaming silver handles. During the next three days people came to pay their respects and then left.

On the Monday Koiki was solemnly buried on a hill at Las with his ancestors. The coffin was placed just below ground level in a low-walled vault facing eastwards towards the sea. A heavy marble slab carefully set into the walls was its only cover, except for the handfuls of soil thrown on to the coffin by close relatives.

The following day the carefully wrapped tombstone was again ritually unveiled to pay respect to 'this great man' and to express pleasure and gratitude that he had come home. The grave was surrounded by a one-strand chain border and a flagpole erected at the head of the grave. A new bronze image of Koiki's face had been set into the tombstone. Netta cut the ribbon to

allow the relatives entry to the grave enclosure. She then carefully unveiled the tombstone. The Murray Island flag was raised
and as the flag flew in the breeze, prayers were said and a hymn
sung.

On the day the desecration was discovered, Netta had told the
Australian's Fiona Kennedy: 'At least if it's taken up to Murray
Island I know it will be left alone and looked after up there.
Nobody would do this kind of thing up there.'[3]

She too had put her past bitterness behind her. Murray Island
was once again sanctuary and home to the Mabo family.

That night at the feast to celebrate the tombstone unveiling,
the Meriam assembled to confirm once again the end of the
mourning period. But after the desecration in Townsville, the
process had been elevated to a new level of ritual significance
for the Meriam elders. The focus was a Malo dance that reached
back past the missionaries and the other colonialist intruders to
the time when Malo's law prevailed and unified the proud and
independent clans of Mer.

Sadly the ceremony took place against a background of
serious dissension among the Meriam people. A group supporting secession from Australia, led by Jim Akee with the support
of the Mer Council of Elders, had set up a Murray Island national
government. They were opposed by the formally elected Murray
Island Council, which had been unsuccessfully ordered off the
island by a directive from Akee, along with the community
police, health workers and teachers in the state primary school,
nearly all of whom were Meriam. The Council retaliated by
passing a resolution disbanding the Council of Elders. Although
his directive was ignored, Akee claimed to have support from
industrialists wishing to explore for oil on the nearby Great
Barrier Reef and he certainly had Meriam supporters on the
island and on the mainland. Akee informed the Australian media,

now very much aware of the symbolic importance of Murray Island, that he was organising a flotilla of boats to allow several hundred Meriam from the mainland to return to Mer in October 1995, one month after the tombstone unveiling. In effect this mass return still has not eventuated and Mr Akee has been found guilty of fraud, in connection with an Islander community organisation he worked for, and given a three-year jail sentence. While this particular demand for secession has come to nothing, it would be foolish to underestimate the desire for increased autonomy within the Torres Strait in general and Mer in particular. Against this background of social and political tension on the mainland and on the island, the Mabo tombstone unveiling provided the Meriam with the opportunity to focus on their oneness as a people, but the conflicting aspirations sometimes surfaced in the public addresses and in interviews given to the media.[4] Factionalism was intense on the island and resulted in a large number of resident Meriam not attending the ceremonies which had been organised by the Council of Elders.

One of the grievances was that nothing had happened on Murray Island since it had been granted native title. The roads were still in the deplorable condition Mabo had complained about in 1990, and the uncollected rubbish had accumulated once again. Sam Wailu, a relative of Mabo, criticised the local council and the government:

> When you see the standard of living nothing has improved since the case — there is rubbish everywhere … We ask the Government for money, but we get nothing. Now rather than having the Government telling us what we can and cannot do we must fight for our rights and stand up for ourselves. Title has been won and we must take on Eddie's battle and keep the spirit of my uncle alive in us.[5]

Donald Whaleboat, Mabo's cousin, also lamented the lack of progress since his death: 'Even though he had all these other plaintiffs he was the only bridge from our side to the wider community.'[6]

The cry was not only for effective leadership but the re-emergence of the spirit that had given the Meriam their traditional strength and confidence. And yet at least half the resident population of this tiny island did not attend the funeral or the tombstone unveiling. The old undercurrents of hostility towards mainland Meriam also apparently lived on. On Mer, 'everyone mamoose'.

At Las the great *agud*, Malo, walked with slow, stately dignity out of the darkness of the night into the light of the celebrations of Mabo's tombstone unveiling. His huge turtle-shell head gazed at the Meriam, intimidating them with its awful dignity as he advanced slowly into the circle. He was followed by his two attendants, each holding one cord, *emes*, that linked them to Malo. As Malo symbolically patrolled his domain in the dance, all Meriam eyes were fixed on this awe-inspiring procession.

Sometimes in the past when the dance had been performed, elders say, kerosene lamps would explode, and some would go out and then light up again, reflecting the great *agud*'s presence. Many believed the spirit of Malo was present at Koiki's burial and tombstone unveiling on Mer. The night was disturbed in a way that could have for them no other explanation. The guardian spirits on Mer which take different forms and manifest themselves in different ways were also restless. The Meriam know when they are near; they feel their presence, hear them and sometimes see their shapes moving in or through the bushes. Meriam elders reported the spirit-guardians of Las were very active after Mabo's funeral, challenging strangers, buffeting them with wind-gusts and shaking the rainforest canopy. They made rattling, rushing noises and sounds like dogs barking where there were no dogs. And the night *toli*, small brown birds, took to the air when the spirits approached. Their presence was felt especially when Malo moved with his attendants out of the darkness into the light of the celebrations of the tombstone unveiling.

The Meriam visitors camped at Las for the ceremonies and the resident Wailu family were concerned for the Townsville stonemason, John Fletcher, who had pitched his tent on the rise near the burial site. He too had heard dogs barking but was not alarmed. They eventually persuaded him to join the Meriam camped at a distance from the sacred site associated with Malo.[7]

Mabo had returned to the world of the Meriam. I have no idea how Koiki would have reacted to the belief so many of his kinsmen had of the presence of Malo and guardian spirits at his funeral on Mer. His sister Marinda believed that Malo had given him the strength and ability that some, like George Mye, had recognised in him when he was a small child on Mer.[8] In our discussions he always spoke of Malo with the certainty of faith. I have only recently learnt of the belief of the Meriam in what I have termed guardian spirits and consequently had never discussed this topic with Koiki. There are many ways of knowing the unknowable other dimension to life. What I am sure of is that Koiki Mabo would have wished for no other burial site than the one he now occupies at Las. His turbulent life had ended in extraordinary triumph and he had at last returned home.

Appendix
Genesis — by Koiki Mabo

It was during that time, too, that my dad was able to tell me about our past. We are not what you may call the original Murray Islanders. [We are] original in the sense that we were there before the European arrived. But actually, before the European came, we ourselves migrated from further north, and it is believed that we came from the Trobriand group, the Trobriand Islands of Papua New Guinea. It is believed that our people travelled from there and they wanted to settle on the tip of the cape of the Papuan Peninsula, I think. And, of course, there were a lot of fights and they moved, followed the coast down to some of the other islands along the coast; but they found the natives were so savage, and man-eaters, and they continued to travel south.

Then they went through the Gulf of Papua to the Kiwai district. There all of the brothers found wives. There were seven of them altogether, and they continued their journey. They stayed there for a little while at Kiwai and, of course, their first sons were born in the Kiwai district.

The first children were born in Kiwai district, and then they left and came further south. They heard there was a place, there was an island out on its own and it was a unique place for them to settle. So they travelled south, and they came to Darnley, and from Darnley to Murray.

At Murray they fought with the people that were there before, and, of course, they won the portion of Murray, and that became a Piadram territory.

The Piadram territory extends from the village. If you look at the map of Murray, you'd look at Dam, the boundary of Dam and Mei, and from there it comes right around to Terker and then out to Dauar. This area they claimed, and their descendants are still there today.

The seven brothers who conquered Murray were Zaiar, who was my ancestor, who settled at Las.

Then there was Gorseg or Ipseg, who settled at Wakik who is the ancestor of the Ipsegs on Murray.

Then there was Kokuam. Kokuam was the ancestor of the Marous and the Toik family and Akee family on Murray. There are quite a few of them.

Then there was Geigi. Geigi was [an ancestor] of the well-known councillor in the Torres Strait, George Mye. Actually his Island name is Geigi — it means 'a king trevally'.

Then there was Wez — Wez, who settled at Terker, whose descendants still occupy that area and the gardening land above it. They are Noahs and Barsas. They're the main ones.

Then we've got the sixth brother who is called Zub. Zub means 'a smoke, a smoke through a hollow pipe' — a bamboo tube they use, they call *zub*. He was named after that, and his descendants are the Dargie family and the Mande family[1]; and there are some others as well who occupy Terker; and that's their territory, territory belonging to Zub.

Now there was a last brother. The last of the seven brothers was called Gamalai or Sigar. He settled on Giar Pit on Dauar Island and the descendants of that Sigar are still occupying that territory. They are the Passis, the Tapims, and the Kudubs, and the Billys. They are the descendants of Sigar, or Gamalai, his other name.

Now actually that land, that territory, was claimed for their older brother named Koit; not Koit, Zaiar. Koit was Zaiar's son.

Now, this goes back 15 generations. Now I'm going to go through all the names of Zaiar's descendants who occupied Las and its gardening territories over that time. It is important that we realise that there were some other younger brothers and sisters, but because of Meriam tradition, the eldest son of a particular family remained the heir of whatever properties and clan heritage and *zogo* they had. He remained the head. Therefore, the story I'm going to tell, that I've learnt from my dad, from my father, is only going to be evolving around the elders of those 15 generations who occupied the village of Las and its surrounding territories.

It is important, too, to understand that when I say 15 generations, I mean the 15 generations of the *zogo le*, the sacred people. They were sacred until the missionaries, in 1871, disrupted them. They were 15 generations, [the fifteenth] generation was my grandfather, Mabo. Actually the pronunciation of my name is not Mar-bo. It's actually Ma'bo [with the stress on the second syllable], a faster way of saying Mabo.

Mabo was the fifteenth generation of that clan who settled on Las, and my father was the sixteenth generation, Benny Mabo. And I am Koiki Mabo. I am the seventeenth generation.

And my sons, of course, Eddie and Mal, and my daughters, Maria, Bethel, Gail, Maleta, and my Celuia, my young daughter, Celuia — they are the eighteenth generation. And my sons' and daughters' children, like Eddie's daughter, Bonita Marie, and Maria's son, Royce Tyson Smith, and Bethel's son, Tyron John Leslie Ryan, are the nineteenth generation of the proud warriors who conquered and settled on Mer.[2]

I also had an older sister too, Jessie. Maria Jessie was her full name. She married Ezra Tapau; and, of course, they had a daughter too, Beryl, and they adopted another daughter by the name of Betty. And their children, of course, young Ezra belonging to Wani and young Wez, are also the nineteenth generation of the clan occupation of Las.

*   *

It's time for a little break now. I want to sing a song that was taught by my grandad. It's about our *Agud*, our *zogo*. The song is belonging to the cult of Malo and Bomai and its English interpretation of the song says, 'Oh, my God, that walks at Las and nurses the sacred sites at Las.'

Wai kara Agud
Las ge
Digemli e ya basigli
A A kara Agud gedi sikerem[3]

After Zaiar had settled with his wife and son, Koit, on Murray, he was made to be the *Ait*, the *Ait* of Mer, which means that was the highest position that anyone was able to achieve, and, of course, this position was then handed down to the first son of the generation that followed.

Zaiar's son, Koit, went back to Kiwai and married four women, and he had four wives, and the other three didn't have the babies, but the first one did. And the first son that was born he named him Wame.

Wame, after he became the *Ait,* also married three women, and those three came from Erub, Darnley; the other came from Edgor; and the third one came from Kiwai, from a village that I'm not quite sure of at this stage. I just can't remember.

After Wame, Azo was born from his first wife, from Darnley, and Azo, when he grew up and became the *Ait*, he also married three women. One was from Aurid, the second one from Purma [Coconut Island], and the third wife was a Kiwai. His first son to survive Azo was again Koit.

Koit, in this case we will call him Koit the second, after Zaiar's son, the original Zaiar's son was the first, and this Koit, we'll call him Koit the second. Koit the second married two women, one from Ugar and the other from Masig, Stephen and Yorke Island. His wife who came from Ugar had a son to him and he called him Awasi, and in this case we'll call him Awasi the first.

Awasi, when he became an *Ait*, also had two women, two wives. One was a Mabadauan and another was a Tureture. They are both villages on the Papuan coast.

After Awasi, Zaiar the second was born. He then went across to the Fly River and married two women.

After, Zaiar the second, he had a son; Zaiar the second had a son and he called him Kokuam.

Kokuam went to Darnley and married his first wife. The second one came from Yorke, Masig, and the third one came from Aurid, and the fourth one, of course, came from Kiwai. His first wife from Erub bore him a son, and he called him Oroto.

Oroto was the first one to have married a woman in the Murray group. He had two wives. The first one came from Waier, and the second one came from Ugar, Stephen Island.

Oroto's first wife bore him a son too, and Oroto called him Misi or Wez. After Misi had grown up and became an *Ait*, he married two women, one from a village close to Saibai, called Buzi, and the other one, along the coast further east, called Sui. They were both Kiwai women.

Now Misi's first wife from Buzi bore him a son, and he called him Awasi or Sam. He had two names, Awasi or Sam, and he married three women. He had three wives and they all came from the Kiwais.

After Awasi or Sam, he had a son, and he called him Waiwai Sam. Sam in my language means the 'cassowary', and the Waiwai means the 'untrimmed feathers of the cassowary'. Now, he also had two wives, and they were from Darnley and Stephen Island, (Ugar).

At this time, for some reason or other, it was decided then that the next generation of the *Ait* was to be a full-blood Meriam. And almost at the same time, the missionaries, I think, must have been in the Pacific; and perhaps Cook or Torres had sailed through Torres Straits. I'm not quite sure, but it seems like that.

Now Awasi's son, Waiwai Sam, was the last *Ait* who married women from other islands.

Now Zaiar the third was born. He also had several brothers, but his wife was known to us as Koket. Koket just means 'a walking stick, a stick that you lean on' — actually 'a leaning stick', but we take it as 'a walking stick'.

His wife, Koket, was the first Meriam *neur,* woman, to have married the *Ait*. Now, she came from a tribe known as Meuram, Meuram tribe, on the northeast of Mer, and their totem is the turtle. There are two totems. One is the turtle, the other one is a seabird. I can't remember the English name, but anyway I'll think about it later.

Now Koket, because she was the eldest of that particular tribe, and came from the eldest brother of the Meuram tribe, inherited quite a lot of land. Quite a lot of land means something like ten acres, approximately ten acres from my judgement, and that land is still being occupied by myself — still being used and owned, traditionally owned, by me.

Now that was Zaiar the third. Now Zaiar the third had a son and he called him Koit, and in this case we call him Koit the third.

Koit also had four wives. His first wife was Anai who came from Zagareb tribe, his second wife came from Waier, and his third wife came from Aurid (I'm not quite sure — Aurid, I think), and the fourth one also came from Papua. Now it was during that time that, we believe, there was the presence of Europeans in that area, according to stories that I learnt about the Salmes. Salmes were [South Sea] Islanders from other islands who landed on Murray and Koit mustered all his Piadram people and they went out to defend their Island.

Koit and his first wife, Anai, were shot — fell the victim of the muskets. Now, before Anai and Koit died, Anai had bore him several sons. The first one was Misi; the second one was Oroto; the third one was Mabo; the fourth one was Beni; and the fifth from his fourth wife, Dobam, who came from the Areb tribe — yes, I remember now — from the Samsep people. Dobam came from there, and she bore him a son called Waiwai Sam.

Now, Misi had a boy. After Koit had [fallen], all his wives remarried.

The two of his wives got married, the ones that didn't have his babies, but the fourth one, Dobam, took all the boys after she had remarried a man, a Komet man by the name of Bauba. She married him and went to live at Sebeg, and, of course, the children, the boys, were still young.

There was an older *zogo le* wanted to initiate someone in their place, in Koit's place, but his own sons were not old enough to be initiated to the position of *Ait*, so they looked around and found Pasi was of a right age, who was the descendant of Gamalai or Sigar, the last brother of Zaiar the first. They took him from Dauar to Mer and they initiated him and he became the *Ait*.

This was only for the time being until Misi or Mabo would have reached the right age, but, of course, this didn't happen.

It happened in a kind of unofficial way, but it was during that time the Europeans had established their presence permanently in the Torres Straits.

All the wives of Koit the third married again, the three remaining ones. I can't remember the names. I know Kak and Dobam had remarried and the fourth one (I can't remember her name). They had remarried, and because the boys were of a very young age, Dobam took them with her to a place where she and her husband lived; and they reared their children up until they were old enough.

And, of course, Misi was initiated first, and Misi became very sick. He was initiated by the remaining *zogo le* that was there, and then Misi got very sick and someone had to occupy Misi's place and they initiated Mabo.

And then it was during that time that it was difficult to move Pasi back to Dauar to be the *Ait* of Dauar because the London Missionary Society had already established its headquarters there on Murray.

And, of course, Pasi had a job as an interpreter for the Samoan missionaries, and he stayed permanently on Murray; and, until now, his descendants, Sam, David, George and the rest, are still on Murray.

Now, on Misi's side, the first son of Koit the third, Misi, only had one boy and one girl. They both married and had no children themselves.

Kaikai, Modi's son, married and he adopted two children, but, of course, the children went back to their own people after he died.

And my mother was a second daughter of Mabo and married a fellow by the name of Robert Zezou Sambo and I am the last of the five children they had.

After our mother died in childbirth, my dad then handed me over to my uncle, to my maternal uncle, Benny Mabo, who was the son, the only son, of Mabo, and they reared me up.

And, of course, Mabo's other brother, Beni, also didn't have any children, and their fourth brother, Oroto, had children himself. His first son was Captain Oth, who became one of the first missionaries that graduated from the College on Mer. And then he married a Murray Island woman, and had a few sons and daughters.

But William Oth was his first son, and William also had several children, and at this stage we're only concentrating on the eldest, so, therefore, Walter Oth now lives in Townsville as William Oth's first son.

Kura or Waiwai Sam, Mabo's last brother from another mother, also had several children, and the first boy in that family was Geary, Geary the first, and he also has a son now.

He has a son and he lives down at Mackay. His name is Geary Mataika.

I spent this day in TVilla Hospital. The Night Netta Malita & Krystle came to see me —

Marriott, Wanee & their families came to see me one night but I dont remember exactly which night. I advised all of them on the problems I was having health wise. I said to all of them please take my Advice and Stop taking foreign matters into your bodies such as Tobacco, Cigarettes, Alcohol and other forms of unnecessary drugs. Tea & Coffee could be the same.
Do not ever get annoyed if your love ones expresses their concerns about your drinking or smoking habits, especially when they ask you to Stop Smoking or Stop Drinking Grog. Because such concerns are made out of Love, they love you so much that they dont want you to ruin your self with dreadful drugs such as the ones mentions Above.

I said to Mum one day, "Oh you dont Love me any more that any you dont buy any more smokes for me. She bust out into tears straightaway and she said, "Oh no it not that Koiki, You know, too Well that I Love you very much and I dont want to be seen as also killing you with all those drugs. So in the future years do not make me buy you any more drugs or cigarettes because I dont want to kill you with my Love & Kindness. Then from that day on I never asked mum to buy me any more smokes or rubbish which may be bad for my health —

So my advice to all my children, including Marrikk, Wanee, AND EZRA, To all my grandchildren & their children.

Please Dont Smoke or Drink LiquoR, Make 1992 the Starting year, for our Drug Free years that will follow on from Now on

'Make 1992 the starting year, for our drug free years'. This concern for the future of his family and relatives was written in the Townsville General Hospital only weeks before his death. (Mabo Papers, National Library)

Thursday 2   *'ville Hospital.*   *Am.*

I spent that Morning in Hospital by my self until about 10 Am. when Nette came in with Maria. Then they met Eleena and Dr Christiani. Ezra was with Maria. Nette & Marriott did not come that morning. So I told them what the doctor had told me about my health.

The doctor was not so sure whether the trip to Brisbane Radium institute was going to make me better or make me worse, but what ever may happen to me I want all of you to take good care of your Mum, Never Abuse her in any way, but let her be the Central figure in your lives just like Death of us has been in your lives!

I also said that I want the property of Mine + Mums at 23 Hibiscus Street, Cranbrook 4814. I hereby express that that I want my share of the property of Mum so decides to sell, 10% of my shares be divided equally amongst all of my biological children, including Edward Dorala, Maria J. Smith, Bethel E Ryan, Caroline Gail Mabo, Malcolm Mabo, Maleta Kuan West and Mahalia Celula Mabo. and also the same percentage (%) to Wanee, Marryat Mabo Snr and Ezra Mabo. Benji Mabo whom I classify as my son, and not as my Grandson. — It must be understood that while this house in 23 Hibiscus Street remains in both of our names. None of my children named above will have a right to force mum to sell out prematurely or for any reason what so ever. The final decision will be hers and hers alone. Even to the point of giving her shares to the children, on the basis similar to what I have decided on my shares.

Or perhaps she might "Will" that property to a company known as "MABO Holding" which would included will be the land claimed in High Court of Aust by Mabo or Mabo's on MER Is (Murray Is) 1981 – 1991.

6/1/92

An entry written in the Townsville General Hospital and completed in hospital in Brisbane. It is signed E.K. Mabo and dated 6 January 1992, two weeks before he died. (Mabo Papers, National Library)

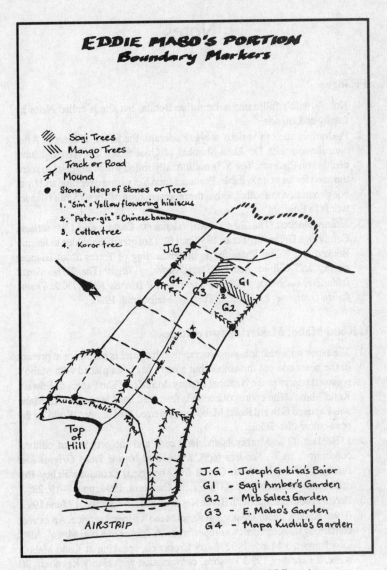

EDDIE MABO'S PORTION
Boundary Markers

Soqi Trees
Mango Trees
Track or Road
Mound
Stone, Heap of Stones or Tree
1. "Sim" = Yellow flowering hibiscus
2. "Pater-giz" = Chinese bamboo
3. Cotton tree
4. Koror tree

J.G
G4
G3
G1
G2
K
3

Private Track

Avenue-Public Road

Top of Hill

AIRSTRIP

J.G — Joseph Gokisa's Baier
G1 — Saqi Amber's Garden
G2 — Meb Salee's Garden
G3 — E. Mabo's Garden
G4 — Mapa Kudub's Garden

Used in High Court Challenge (Mabo Papers, National Library)

Notes

Prologue

1. Koiki's wife's full name is Ernestine Bonita, but she is called Netta by family and friends.
2. Piadram is spelt in various ways: Piaderam, Piadaram, Paiderem. After consultation with Dr Anna Shnukal of Queensland University, I have decided on Piadram. The 'r' is traditionally rolled which suggests to some the need for an extra syllable. Pronunciation has varied over time and from one generation to another, as has the representation of Torres Strait Islander words in English.
3. Jeremy Beckett, *The Torres Strait Islanders: Custom and Colonialism*, Cambridge University Press, 1987, p. 112. I am greatly beholden to Jeremy Beckett and Nonie Sharp for an understanding of Torres Strait Islander history and culture. See N. Sharp, *Stars of Tagai: The Torres Strait Islanders*, Canberra, 1993 and *Torres Strait Islands 1879–1979: Theme for an Overview*, La Trobe University, Melbourne, 1980.

1. Koiki Mabo: Mastering two cultures

1. The tapes on which this autobiographical material is based are at present in the possession of the author, but a copy has been placed with Mabo's personal papers in the National Library, MS8822: 'The Papers of Edward Koiki Mabo'. The entire collection is restricted until January 2005. Mabo was baptised Edward Koiki Mabo but preferred the Islander 'Koiki' to the post-colonialist 'Eddie'.
2. J. Beckett, 'The Murray Island land case and the problem of cultural continuity', in W. Sanders (ed.), *Mabo and Native Title: Origins and Institutional Implications*, Centre for Aboriginal Economic Policy Research, Australian National University, Canberra, 1994, pp. 17–19, 22.
3. Personal conversation with Bryan Keon-Cohen, Townsville, 17 June 1993.
4. Bryan Keon-Cohen, speaking at Koiki Mabo's funeral service. An extract containing this comment was repeated in 'A Tribute to Koiki Mabo', ABC Law Report, 3 March 1992. Larry Cromwell, speaking at Koiki Mabo's wake, 2 February 1992. Personal conversation with Henry Reynolds, 20 July 1994.
5. *Worker's Weekly*, 24 September 1931. See also M. Franklin, *Black and White Australians: An Inter-Racial History 1788–1975*, Heinemann Educational Australia, South Yarra, Melbourne, 1976, p. 134. Economic and

legal equality for Aborigines was included in the Communist Party's 1943 platform and its members were urged to support Aboriginal advancement.

6. C. Rowley, *The Remote Aborigines,* Ringwood, Penguin, 1972, pp. 106-108.

7. K. Orr (ed.), *We the Australians: What Is to Follow the Referendum?,* Townsville, 1967, pp. 1, 33.

8. Loos, informal discussion over the years. See also Beckett, 'The Murray Island land case and the problem of cultural continuity', pp. 19–23. A.C. Haddon (ed.), *Reports of the Cambridge Anthropological Expedition to Torres Strait,* six volumes, Cambridge University Press, 1908–1935, especially vol.VI, *Sociology, Magic and Religion of the Eastern Islanders.*

9. See H. Reynolds (ed.), *Race Relations in North Queensland,* Department of History and Politics, James Cook University, Townsville, 1993, pp. 2–3, for Reynolds' account of this interaction. The reason for the lunch is lost in time. It was possibly in association with the oral history project Reynolds and I were launching. Mabo was our first Research Assistant. Reynolds thinks it was just to have lunch. Personal conversation, 3 August 1994.

10. N. Sharp, 'Springs of originality among the Torres Strait Islanders: after the storm winds the leafing of the wongai tree', PhD thesis, La Trobe University, Melbourne, 1984, vol. II, 'Book of Islanders', p. 136. I participated in this conference but was not in the discussion group where Koiki 'did his dance'.

11. J. Morris, 'The Black Community School', unpublished assignment, Department of History and Politics, pp. 9–11. See *Townsville Daily Bulletin,* 14, 17, 19, 21 September 1973; 6 April 1974.

12. Address of Ms Lois O'Donoghue, Chairperson, Aboriginal and Torres Strait Islander Commission, at inaugural meeting of Torres Strait Regional Authority, 1 July 1994. The copy was supplied by ATSIC through Senator Margaret Reynolds' office. Torres Strait Regional Authority, *Corporate Plan 1994–95* [ATSIC, Canberra], 1994.

13. *Townsville Bulletin,* 24 May 1994.

14. J. Griffin (ed.), *The Torres Strait Border Issue: Consolidation, Conflict or Compromise?,* Townsville College of Advanced Education, Townsville, 1976, pp. 34–5. Personal discussion with Mabo revealed he had these views well before the 1976 conference which I attended. S.J. Kehoe-Forutan, *Torres Strait Independence: A Chronicle of Events,* Research Report no.1, Department of Geographical Sciences, University of Queensland, St Lucia, Qld, July 1988, pp. 11–31.

15. Koiki Mabo, report on audiocassette of a visit to Thursday Island, April 1973, given to Noel Loos by Henry Reynolds. Mabo was collecting oral history for Reynolds and Loos. On this tape Mabo reads a telegram he had

sent to George Mye, a leading figure on Darnley Island, advising him not to trust or support Bjelke-Petersen. See Griffin (ed.), *The Torres Strait Border Issue: Consolidation, Conflict or Compromise*, for an account of the issues involved in the Border dispute, especially pp. 34–35 for Mabo's views.

16. Chairman, Murray Island Council, to Edward Mabo, 17 October 1974, telegram: 'Permission granted to visit your father stop You will never undertake political affairs stop Please acknowledge and confirm'. In possession of Bonita Mabo. 'Never' was interpreted by Bonita Mabo as meaning during his visit.

17. Eddie Koiki Mabo, 'Land rights in the Torres Strait' (pp. 143–48) and Barbara Hocking, 'Is might right? An argument for the recognition of traditional Aboriginal title to land in the Australian Courts' (pp. 207–22) in E. Olbrei (ed.), *Black Australians: The Prospects for Change*, James Cook University of North Queensland Student Union, Townsville. See also Greg McIntyre, Aboriginal Land Rights — a definition at Common Law' (pp. 222–23) and 'Resolutions 20–24' (pp. 247–48).

18. Morris, The Black Community School, pp. 9–11. See *Townsville Daily Bulletin*, 14, 17, 19, 21 September 1973; 6 April 1974.

19. Beckett, 'The Murray Island land case and the problem of cultural continuity', pp. 19–23.

20. Maiga Mabo to Bonita Mabo, present date [prior to September 1960], Box 2, File 1, MS8822, National Library: 'The Papers of Edward Koiki Mabo'. I have made some minor editorial changes to the texts of both letters. It is customary for Torres Strait Islanders of these generations to address each other quite formally in English.

21. Maiga Mabo, Murray Island, to Bonita Mabo, 23 November 1960, Box 2, File 1, MS8822, National Library: 'The Papers of Edward Koiki Mabo'.

22. Koiki Mabo, *Diary*, 5 May 1989, Mabo Papers. I was introduced to Marinda Mareko in Townsville on 6 August 1995 at the National Library's launching of *Guide to the Papers of Edward Koiki Mabo*. She told me proudly, without any questioning or prompting from me, that she was Koiki's sister. It was a very brief, informal conversation.

23. Writ No.1594 of 1986, Supreme Court of Queensland, Justice Moynihan, Brisbane, between Eddie Mabo, David Passi and James Rice, Plaintiffs, and State of Queensland and Commonwealth of Australia, and *Mabo v. Queensland and the Commonwealth*, Supreme Court of Queensland, Moynihan J, 16 November 1990, *Determination Pursuant to Reference of 27 February 1986 by the High Court of Australia to hear and determine all issues of fact raised by the pleadings, particulars and further particulars in High Court Action B12 of 1982*.

24. The Iris Clay Hostel was opened on 12 July 1975. I thought Koiki's return to the Christian faith was evident at Maleta Mabo's wedding on 1 October 1988. Bonita and Maleta think it occurred as late as 1990. I can remember Koiki inviting me to Torres Strait Islander church services which were open to all denominations. In my mind, this seems earlier than 1990, and not long after the October 1988 wedding. In 1980, when interviewed by Nonie Sharp, Koiki Mabo had remarked: 'I don't place very much emphasis on hymns; it's not my thing.' See Sharp, 'Springs of originality among the Torres Strait Islanders', vol. II, p. 137.

25. 'A tribute to Koiki Mabo', ABC Law Report, 3 March 1992. The funeral proceedings were recorded in full by the Townsville Aboriginal and Islander Media Association.

2. Growing up on Murray Island

1. The Miriam was transcribed and translated by Donald Whaleboat, Koiki's cousin, and Elemo Tapim. The Kala Laga Ya was transcribed and translated by Dana Ober. I have used Dana's free translation with some words from his literal translation.

2. Dr Nonie Sharp, a sociologist at La Trobe University who has done extensive research in the Torres Strait.

3. See 'Genesis: an Epilogue'.

4. Mabo actually said 'that white beliefs were the only ones', but at this time there was considerable distraction caused by grandchildren, background music and the Mabo dog. It is clear that he meant 'that white beliefs were *not* the only ones'.

5. Esra is an alternative form of Asera.

3. Coming to grips with white-man culture

1. This interview was recorded in November 1984.

2. Burnum Burnum lived in Townsville for a number of years and was committed to the Aboriginal advancement and land rights movement. We knew him then as Harry Penrith. He became a close friend of Koiki Mabo and the Loos family and was a frequent visitor to both our homes. He still drops in when he is in North Queensland with fascinating accounts of his latest exploits, plans, ideas and controversies.

3. This statement was on a cassette supplied to me by Mrs Bonita Mabo in 1994. The original is now in the Mabo papers. I have a copy.

4. Changing ways

1. Maureen Fuary is an anthropologist at James Cook University whose research has focused on the Torres Strait Islanders, including the use of sorcery. Koiki had attended her discussion on the use of sorcery on one Torres Strait Island, along with some other Torres Strait Islander students, one of whom came from that island and knew the alleged but unnamed sorcerers.

2. Some years ago I was aware of vague rumours that *pouri-pouri* was practised or feared in Townsville. I have recently been informed by a Meriam man that it is still practised.

6. Being black in North Queensland

1. See 'Genesis: an epilogue'.

7. Netta

1. Remon Geesu was best man at Koiki and Netta's wedding.
2. Nicey Sambo is Koiki Mabo's older brother. He wasn't adopted by Benny and Maiga Mabo.

8. A very active activist

1. Koiki Mabo, Diary, 4 October 1991, Mabo Papers, National Library. See also *Diary*, 26 January 1989. See also National Library, *Guide to the Papers of Edward Koiki Mabo*, Canberra, 1995, p. 7. Some minor editorial changes and corrections have been made to excerpts from the Mabo Papers.

2. E.K. Mabo to Department of Health, Queensland, 29 December 1990. There is a handwritten draft of his application for one of three positions advertised in *Weekend Australian*, 22–23 December 1990 by the Queensland Department of Health. There are also several typed undated copies of his application. It is ironic that Mabo was applying for positions within the Queensland Government at a time when he was the leading litigant against it in the native title case. Interview with Bonita Mabo, Townsville, 12 February 1995.

3. Telephone discussion with Mr Francis Tapim, 29 March 1996.

4. Edward Koiki Mabo, 'Draft Proposal for the Establishment of the Magani Institute', 7 August 1978, Australian Institute of Aboriginal and Torres Strait Islander Studies. Copy supplied by the Principal, Dr W. Jonas.

5. Edward Koiki Mabo, Application for Research Grant & Referee Report Sheets, Australian Institute of Aboriginal Studies, 18 November 1984,

approved 30 November 1984. Copy supplied by the Principal, Dr W. Jonas. I have corrected the spelling of some words, one in my own extract.

6. E.K. Mabo to Secretary, Fish Management Authority, 7 January 1991, draft, Mabo Papers.

7. Koiki Mabo, Diary, 9 May 1991; E.K. and E.B. Mabo to The Manager, [n.d.] Mabo Papers. This is a circular letter requesting an eight-week work experience to accompany the Bookkeeping and Accounting Course at Concord Tax. Koiki and Bonita were in receipt of a Commonwealth Government Training Grant.

8. See Koiki Mabo, Diaries, 1985, 1987, 1988, 1991, 1992, Mabo Papers. There are no diaries for 1986 and 1990. There are many gaps in the existing diaries.

9. George Mye, Darnley Island, telephone conversation, 17 October 1995.

10. Moynihan, Determination, p. 67.

11. Mabo, Diary, 28 May 1989.

12. Koiki Mabo, Diary, 7 January 1989, Mabo Papers. He planted yams and cassava at 'top end of Bohle near the golf link[s]'.

13. Discussion with Netta Mabo and his daughter, Maleta West, 13 February 1995. Adult Education Enrolment Form, Townsville College of TAFE, 10 July 1991, Mabo Papers. There are also a number of diary entries indicating he was 'working on the boat'.

14. Koiki Mabo, Diary, 22 April 1991, 14 May 1991; *Age*, 13 January 1995.

15. Koiki Mabo, Diary, 19–24 February 1991.

16. Affidavit in the Supreme Court of Queensland at Townsville *in the matter of* the Community Services (Torres Strait) Act of 1984 as amended and *in the matter* of an Election for the Island Council for Murray Island Scheduled for the 23rd day of March 1991 and *in the matter* of an Application by *Edward Koiki Mabo* [copy], dated March 1991, Mabo Papers. Discussion with Bonita Mabo, Townsville, 17 February 1995, and Mr Dale Treanor, the Cairns lawyer who prepared the affidavit, 21 March 1995.

17. Ibid.

18. Ibid. No diary has yet been found for 1990 when Mabo was at Murray Island.

19. Yarra Bank Films (Sharon Connolly and Trevor Graham), *Land Bilong Islanders*, Ronin Films, Canberra, 1990.

20. Koiki Mabo, 1988 Diary, 31 December 1987. This entry is on one of the 'Notes' pages. 'Duri' is spelt 'Dure' in 'Murray Island: Sketch Map. Eddie Mabo's Land Group 3: Goi lands. Statement of Claims: para 5(a)(iv)', Mabo Papers.

21. Koiki Mabo, Diary, 24 March 1991, Mabo Papers.

22. E. Mabo and Others, Murray Island Land Claim, undated copy, Mabo Papers. The letter refers to 1 and 15 October 1986.
23. Roberta Sykes, 'After Eddie', *HQ Magazine*, March/April 1995, pp .73–74.
24. Koiki Mabo, Diary, 2 January 1988, Mabo Papers.
25. Ibid., 3 January 1988, Mabo Papers.
26. Netat Urapun Buai Progressive Association, Policy Discussion Paper on Road Improvements [n.d.], Mabo Papers. There is also an earlier draft.
27. Koiki Mabo, Diary, 19 May 1989, Mabo Papers.
28. Ibid., 20 May 1989.
29. Ibid., 21 May 1989.
30. Ibid., 12 January, 18–20 January 1988.
31. Ibid., 1 July 1985.
32. Untitled welcome speech for First National Conference, 22–25 June 1991, Mabo Papers. 'Iina' is Western Island Language, *Kala Laga Ya*, for 'here' which is understood throughout the Torres Strait. The name implies at a more literal level that Torres Strait Islanders live 'here'. The organisation of that name is in Brisbane and is proudly asserting its presence as a Torres Strait Islander organisation in the urban situation. At another level it says to Torres Strait Islander people 'here to stay' and is an assertion of Torres Strait Islander identity. (Discussion with John Whop, 28 February 1995.)
33. Discussion with Bonita Mabo, 14 February 1995.
34. Koiki Mabo, Diary, 15 March 1988, M.P. 'Agud' is also spelt 'Augud', especially in Kala Laga Ya, and means 'totem' or 'god'.
35. This was the conference organised by the Townsville Treaty Committee and James Cook University Students' Union. See E. Olbrei (ed.) *Black Australians: The Prospects for Change*. Papers and discussions from the national conference, 'Land Rights and the Future of Australian Race Relations', Students' Union, James Cook University, Townsville, 1981, passim.
36. *Sydney Morning Herald*, 30 April 1985, 'Islanders take white Australia to the High Court', by David Monaghan.
37. Pamphlet 'Islanders take white Australia to the High Court', Mabo Papers. There is also a handwritten mock-up.
38. 'Qld acts to head off High Court', *Sydney Morning Herald* [n.d.] containing Mabo's statement in Meriam Mir and English.
39. E.K. Mabo, ' "Historic benchmark" for Aborigines, Islanders', 16 April 1985, Mabo Papers.
40. Koiki Mabo, Diary, 4 November 1991, Mabo Papers.
41. Ibid., 27–28 November 1991.
42. High Court of Australia, Eddie Mabo and Ors, Plaintiffs, and the State of Queensland, Dependant, 3 June 1992, F.C. 92/014, 'Order'.

43. Koiki Mabo, Diary, 1992, written on a 'Notes' page on 4 January 1992, Mabo Papers.

44. Ibid. The entry is dated 6 January 1992 and signed 'E. Mabo' but is at 2 January 1992 in the diary.

45. This entry was made in the week before his death, probably on Sunday, 19 January. He died on 21 January 1992.

46. Ibid. This entry, made in the first two weeks of 1992 before Koiki went to Brisbane for radium treatment, is entered under 31 December 1991, in one of the introductory pages to the 1992 Diary.

9. Return to Mer

1. Discussion with Donald Whaleboat, 16 June 1996.

2. With kind permission of Trevor Graham, Film Australia, 'National Interest Program', 'E.K. Mabo', Roll No. 15. This copy is in possession of Mrs Bonita Mabo. This and other rushes are being used in the production of a documentary on Mabo's life, 'Koiki'.

3. *Australian*, 5 June 1995, p. 1.

4. See for example Marcus Priest, 'Promise of Mabo lost in Paradise', *Courier-Mail*, 23 September 1995, pp. 1, 12, 13.

5. *Ibid.*, p. 1.

6. *Ibid.*

7. Discussion with Donald Whaleboat and Elemo Tapim, Netta Mabo and other family members during 1995 and with John Fletcher, a Townsville stonemason, and Donald Whaleboat, 27 May 1996.

8. Discussion with Trevor Graham, 3 June 1996.

Genesis: an epilogue

1. Mande, now spelt Monday. In this section, the earliest forms of spelling have been used.

2. Bonita supplied more recent details of her and Koiki's family members (as of November 1995). Members of the eighteenth generation (Koiki's and her children) are numbered, followed in brackets by their children, the Mabo grandchildren, being the nineteenth generation.

    1. Eddie (Bonita Marie MABO)

    2. Jessie Maria (Royce Tyson, Desai, Steven and Tyler SMITH)

    3. Bethel (Tyron John Leslie and Nathan Zaia RYAN; Jordan Ashley DUNCAN)

    4. Caroline Gail (Kaleb Michael, Joel Graham, William Koiki and Rebecca Leigh MABO-COHAN)

5. Mahalingham (known as <u>Mal</u>) (Joseph, Maria Jean, Lionel Segedam, Naomi Maiga, Katherine Akazi and Halie David MABO)
6. <u>Maleta</u> (Krista Jade and Megan Kayle WEST)
7. <u>Celuia</u> (Brian Edward MABO)

Adopted children of Koiki and Bonita Mabo

8. <u>Wanee</u> Beryl (Wesley, Cassandra, Jessie Mai, Merinda Evon)
9. <u>Ezra</u> Benny
10. <u>Mario</u>

3. This haunting verse is repeated four times. Koiki sings it beautifully.